Awaken Your Inner Goddess

AWAKEN YOUR INNER GODDESS

Practical Tools for Self-Care,
Emotional Healing,
and Self-Realization

DR. DARA GOLDBERG, PHD

ROCKRIDGE
PRESS

Interior and Cover Designer: Francesca Pacchini
Art Producer: Sara Feinstein
Editor: Samantha Barbaro
Production Editor: Rachel Taenzler
Illustrations used under license from Shutterstock.com.

ISBN: Print 978-1-64739-114-0 | eBook 978-1-64739-115-7

R1

This book is dedicated to anyone who
would like to reconnect with their authentic
self, transcend difficult circumstances,
foster healthy connections, help heal
planet Earth, and fully embrace their inner
light. It is with gratitude that I honor those
who have embodied intuitive feminine
energy through darkness, providing a
guiding light for others to find their own way.
May this book reach you in divine timing.

CONTENTS

Introduction: You Are a Divine Spiritual Being

HELLO AND WELCOME.

In this moment, we have connected—my energy and yours. I am here to help you hold sacred space for your growth process as you rediscover your unique spark. Together, we will go inward to identify obstacles, fears, or shadows that may be blocking your divine inner light. It is time to step into your power.

I'm honored to be here with you. As a clinical psychologist who specializes in working with women to help them live in their true light at any stage of the life cycle, I have a deep understanding of what it takes, both spiritually and psychologically, to heal and discover the divine being within all of us. After decades of learning and seeking inner balance, I discovered how to trust my strength and internal guidance. Today I accept only healthy support, even when it comes from mysterious places. Now I want to help you do the same: to align with your true self—perhaps after a long disconnect, or maybe for the first time.

From both a spiritual and evidence-based psychological perspective, I offer exercises and tools that can help you discover your truest self and protect your energy. However, I am only here as a guide. Your path is your own. You have permission to keep what you find helpful, and release what you do not. The goal is for you to feel comfortable and nurture yourself—and this looks different for everyone.

The path of healing we explore in this book is based on the concept of a divine source. This source is always within you and always accessible. It is the embodiment of your spirituality—whether that takes the form of religion or something more specific to your own journey, even simply whatever moves you, inspires you, or gives you hope. Often when we lose our way in life, we've lost touch with this source. But you can always find it again. Processing any stuck points or psychological, emotional, and energetic wounding can help you get there. This is the kind of healing and self-renewing work we'll do together.

I've divided this book into three parts. In part 1, I'll help you look inward and figure out where you are in terms of knowing your true authentic light. Perhaps you are already living in full alignment with this light—if so, great! This book will still provide opportunities for self-reflection and growth. Or perhaps you've lost your way and are yearning for a helping hand to guide you home. This book is here for you. We'll also do some exercises to identify possible barriers that might be holding you back. As you work through this book, I recommend keeping a special journal and pen nearby. Writing is a vital form of self-discovery, and I've included prompts for journaling throughout the book.

Once you've gotten in touch with who you are, we'll move to part 2, which provides guidance for cocreating your path forward with your divine source and figuring out where you want to go. This is deep, important work. If at any point you feel overwhelmed, you can set the book down, take a break, and return at any time.

Finally, in part 3, I'll help you create realistic and achievable goals to get where you want to go and to care for yourself along the way. During this process, you'll allow your true self to emerge.

While you are wonderful just as you are, this three-part process of discovery and healing will help you tap into your true potential, feel centered, and step into the future with a deeper sense of self.

Throughout the book, we'll call on goddess spirituality, both from within us and around us. I'll help you identify and tap into your own divine gifts, and pull strength from and embody goddess archetypes from throughout mythology and history. Whether harnessed from within or around you, goddess energy is a conduit for your personal power and the collective power of women. It is always there for you to tap into and embrace as part of your path toward your most authentic self.

Now let's bring in the sun!

PART **ONE**

WHO YOU ARE

Your journey toward your true self begins by awakening your own empowerment. In this section, we'll explore how you can look inward, recognize your strengths, and tap into your divine gifts. You'll learn about your true authentic light and how to let it shine. We'll also talk about how support for and from other women plays a key role in your well-being and healing, and the well-being of all women. So, let's get started!

CHAPTER **ONE**

Get in Touch with Yourself

This chapter will help you connect to your inner divinity, or spiritual self. We will peel back the layers of past experiences to uncover what lies beneath. The better you get to know yourself, the more balanced and secure you'll feel. This way, no matter what's going on around you, you can feel safe within your own eye of the storm. As you become more self-aware, you will also be empowered to accept your divine gifts—your bright, shining, internal sun! Warm, glowing, strong, and centered, it is always there to guide you.

The Spiritual Self

WHAT EXACTLY IS our spiritual self? Think of it as a divine spark that lives within us at all times. Even if it has been shadowed by life experiences, that spark is still there, waiting to shine through. Connecting to your spiritual self is integral to the healing and therapeutic practices in this book. I've found that helping women rediscover and reclaim their spiritual self gives them a north star to guide them back to the life they want to live, the life that feels good and true.

For many, the most important step on this journey is to heal stuck points, old wounds, or traumas that may be caught in the body and blocking your inner light. This means processing information held within the energy systems in your body, such as your auric layers (relating to your aura), chakra system, and subtle energy bodies. Even if we cannot see, feel, or sense them, these systems are always processing our experiences on an energetic level. Let's take a quick look (I encourage you to do further research on energy systems if you're intrigued, as they are incredibly powerful—see Resources on page 167):

The aura is an invisible energetic field that surrounds all living beings. The colors of your aura represent the nuances of your spiritual well-being. Auras can have a different combination of colors, and your aura can change. It is said that there are seven auric layers and that they connect with the chakra system.

Chakras are the energy centers in the body. When our chakras are open, energy can move freely throughout the body, creating balance and harmony. When our chakras are blocked, we also experience a blockage in our physical, emotional, or spiritual well-being. The seven chakras are the root chakra (red), sacral chakra (orange), solar plexus chakra (yellow), heart chakra (green/pink), throat chakra (blue), third eye chakra (indigo), and crown chakra (violet/white).

Subtle energy bodies are layers of energy that radiate outward from our physical bodies. These layers compose our energetic field.

Whether we have conscious awareness of it or not, these energy systems can hold trauma, wounding, and even illness. The good news is that we can cleanse these energy systems and replenish them with new energy. To do this, you must welcome your full self into the light, especially your shadow elements, to illuminate and clear any blockages.

Self-Awareness

WHEN WE BECOME more self-aware, we're able to decipher defense mechanisms or dysfunctional belief systems and patterns that originally developed as coping mechanisms to keep us safe but now hold us back. For example, if you grew up in a chaotic home, you may have learned to disassociate, or detach yourself, during stressful moments in order to feel safe in that environment. But continuing this pattern of dissociation in your adult relationships can prevent you from true connection with others.

Traumas, core wounds, energetic blocks, energetic connections to others, and the projections of others may all be entangled in your perception of yourself. To reach true self-awareness, it's important to remove everything that is attached to you but is not actually yours or no longer serves you.

Your true self is more than your body, your thoughts, behaviors, or emotions. Your body is your vessel. Your thoughts, behaviors, and emotions are products of experiences. Your true self is separate from all this—it is pure, wise, and removed from external circumstance and pain. It emanates from your soul, spirit, or heart center. The more you connect to your true self, the more you will understand your actions and reactions, and the more control you will have in creating your life experience.

If you've experienced a trauma, symptoms such as intrusive thoughts, intense memories, sudden emotions, or frightening dreams may feel out of your control. These symptoms arise because the traumatic experience was too upsetting to comprehend or process at the time. It lives within you and continues to affect you and how you relate to the world. The trauma remains in your emotional, mental, physical, and energetic bodies—blocking your connection to self. Your mind is constantly attempting to grasp the meaning of the event and integrate it with your understanding of what you know to be true. An unimaginable hardship can raise deeper questions about the meaning of life and why things happen. This can shake your sense of internal peace and can cause unsettling feelings of loss of control, absence of purpose, and powerlessness.

When you connect to your core truth within and align with your divinity, you will feel more at peace. This is true regardless of your experiences or the severity of your traumas. Returning home to yourself takes effort and energy, but it gets easier with practice. It is possible for everyone.

A WORD ON TRAUMA

IF YOU HAVE experienced and are recovering from a trauma, you are not alone. According to the Recovery Village, 70 percent of adults in the US experience at least one traumatic event in their lifetime, and 20 percent of people who experience a traumatic event will develop post-traumatic stress disorder (PTSD). About eight million adults in the US suffer from PTSD during a given year. The statistics are even more staggering for women. According to the National Center for PTSD, about 10 percent of women develop PTSD sometime in their life (compared with about 4 percent of men).

If you believe you have suffered a trauma, it's important to acknowledge that trauma and find the help you need through the many available sources of support (see Resources, page 167). The first step is to ask for help. Healing traumas is a foundational part of the process of knowing and becoming yourself. Trauma does not heal on its own. It needs to be uncovered, explored, and processed, often with the help of a professional therapist or counselor.

THERE'S NOTHING WRONG WITH YOU

NO MATTER WHAT you have experienced, there is nothing wrong with you. Take a moment to let that soak in: *There is nothing wrong with you.* While we may not be able to control everything that happens to us, what is in our control is how we respond and heal. Life experiences are part of being human and do not determine your value.

Your eternal self is whole and complete. The strength you need to survive is always within you, even when it seems hard to find. Even when you feel lost, your spiritual self always knows the way home. If you have suffered a traumatic event or loss, you may feel broken down. Support is crucial. You are worthy of receiving the help and support you need. Finding the light at the core of your being can give you the strength to welcome the right support, while also maintaining your own healthy boundaries. Remember that no matter what happens to your physical, mental, or emotional self, your soul is never broken.

Sometimes We Lose Touch with Ourselves, and That's Okay

MANY LIFE CIRCUMSTANCES can distract us from our core truth. A powerful first step toward reclaiming your true light is the recognition that who you are is deeper than what you have experienced, or even what you perceive with your five senses.

It is completely natural to get caught up in the web of daily existence. Jobs, relationships, obligations, ambitions, other people, and material and financial pursuits are all great distractions of the modern world. The goal is not to remove yourself entirely from this collective existence, but to empower your true self to exist within it. Let's take a moment to reflect on the things that are currently distracting you from yourself. Write your answers in your journal so you can come back to them as needed:

What are some things you do to please others that take away from your true self?

What pursuits or stressors in your life right now are taking up too much energy?

Name three ways you could let go of these pursuits or stressors.

How much care do you provide for others who do not have the capacity to reciprocate?

Name three relationships that often leave you feeling depleted.

Name three relationships that leave you feeling empowered and more like yourself.

It's possible to be a caregiver, healer, relative, or friend without taking away from yourself. But you may have to enforce some healthy boundaries. Self-awareness can help you recognize when you are becoming depleted and are in need of self-care. Some signs of depletion include:

- Exhaustion
- Irritability
- Decreased quality of work or play
- Lack of interest in hobbies or activities
- Reacting without full control

Being aware of your signs will help you care for yourself and establish boundaries around the people and things that take you away from yourself. What are your signs? Here's a quiz to help you find out.

ARE YOU DEPLETED?

1. A child asks you an innocent question—for the 10th time in a row. You:

    A. Recognize their sweet innocence and gently inform them that the answer is not going to change, but only after offering a developmentally appropriate explanation.

    B. Firmly tell them to stop asking for the 10th time.

    C. Snap at them to be quiet.

2. Your boss calls you into work at the last minute. You:

    A. Acknowledge the importance of the situation, but take careful consideration of your physical and emotional needs. You agree only to what you can handle in good health.

B. Consider your own need to recharge, but accept anyway out of fear of being disliked or letting down your boss.

C. Immediately agree to do it and then spend the next week complaining about the situation and your boss to your coworkers, friends, and family.

3. You go shopping with your sister. You:

A. Both share your own versions of self-expression.

B. Show her what styles you are considering, but wait for her opinion before making your final purchasing decision.

C. Only choose what she says is currently in fashion because you are not confident in your own self-expression.

4. How is your energy level today? Let's check in with your physiology and assess your adrenal health:

A. You woke up feeling well-rested and ready to go!

B. When 4 p.m. rolls around, you plan to grab a large frozen coffee.

C. You feel stressed and fatigued, and cannot seem to find a healthy way out of this negative feedback loop.

5. You are working on your spiritual self, and you are *not* loving everybody. What do you do?

A. Remind yourself that it's okay to accept your feelings! You don't waste your energy directing negativity toward anyone; instead, you channel it out in a healthy way by refocusing it on your healthy relationships.

B. Spend an hour crying out your hurt feelings, and then give yourself a hug for honoring your emotions. In your journal, you write a mantra about welcoming healthy relationships. You start saving up some compassion, strength, and wisdom for your future self, who will know how to stand tall and be assertive when faced with difficult situations and relationships.

C. You blame yourself and don't have the energy to think of changes you could make in the future.

Mostly As: What you're doing is working! You have a good sense of your needs and enough fuel to act with self-compassion.

Mostly Bs: You know how to refuel, but don't quite have enough in your tank to stay the course. You are beginning to feel depleted. It's time to enforce more time and energy for yourself.

Mostly Cs: Call Athena, the goddess of wisdom and courage! You are depleted and not acting in your own self-interest. Remember that you are worthy of compassion and fiercely set the intention to increase compassion for yourself. Identify opportunities to take more time and energy for yourself, and act on them this week.

THE GODDESS ATHENA

The concept of a goddess can be viewed in terms of an archetype: a constellation of attributes, forces, or values that are timeless and important, and transcend the human experience. As you walk your path, contemplating a goddess archetype may provide encouragement, inspiration, and a feeling of divine support. We'll explore goddess spirituality in the next chapter, but read on to learn more about the goddess Athena.

Named after her city of Athens, this Greek goddess (called Minerva in Roman mythology) is a creatress and goddess of wisdom. Strategic in battle and a protector of heroes, she is often portrayed wearing armor. Her archetype has been an inspiration for individual creativity as well as interpersonal connection through artistry. By her side is the owl, representing wisdom and intuition (the ability to see in the dark). As a warrior goddess, her connection to darkness also symbolizes rebirth and transformation.

It has been said that Athena planted the first olive tree. This sacred tree of the goddess holds many symbolic implications, including peace, hope, and resurrection.

Reach Out to Yourself

THE PROCESS OF reaching out to connect with your true authentic self begins with intention. Not sure where to start? Let's practice. You can do this whenever you have lost sight of who you are, whether due to a painful situation or the myriad distractions of daily life.

Take a deep breath. Hug yourself as you would hug a friend who's having a tough time. Give yourself permission to feel whatever it is you are feeling in this very moment without judgment. No one is allowed to judge you in this moment—not even you—*because you say so*. Right now, by doing this, you are setting healthy boundaries and tending to your emotions.

Now bring awareness to your surroundings. Where are you right now? Are you in a safe place? Are you comfortable? Do you have privacy? Find a safe space where you will not be interrupted for at least 5 to 10 minutes. Get comfortable.

Next, we'll find your safe space within—your own eye of the storm.

"Going within" is the first step in separating external elements from your true self. Whatever is within is yours. You are in control at all times, even if you don't feel like it. For this exercise, I would like you to practice radically accepting—just for this short moment—that you are in full control. Say these words or similar words that feel comfortable to you:

Whatever comes up, I have control. Whatever arises, it is because I am ready to look at it.

Now think practically about the resources you can turn to for support. Think about who you call, where you go, and what you do to stay safe. Remember that these resources are always available to you. They weave together to become your safety net as you go within.

Now visualize a divine source of support. Some examples of support could include your eternal spirit, a fictional character, living person, deceased loved one, higher power, spirit guide, spirit animal, elemental, guardian angel, or archangel. Feel free to invite any image that you would like; just make sure it's one that feels supportive and uplifting.

Now that you have invited in a source of support, envision a protective bubble around yourself to further define your safe space. I want you to feel fully free to explore within your bubble. This is your process. There is no rush. All you have to do now is pay attention as a detached observer.

As the detached observer in full control, you may turn to your visualized source of support at any time. In fact, don't be surprised if this source says something encouraging or offers a gift to help you feel comforted and safe. For example, perhaps you have invited in the image of your grandmother, and she offers you the image of a book you used to read together, the memory of a favorite meal, or even the feeling of a hug.

Now you may welcome in what is ready to come to you. As soon as something comes up for you, imagine holding it in a safe, separate container until you're ready to open it. Imagine the container now—is it a diary with a lock? A box with a key? This can be any type of container that reaffirms your sense of control regarding when and how you will open it.

For this short moment, practice not judging anything. Just feel what comes up. (Any time you feel uncomfortable, your diary, box, or container is there—you hold the key at all times!) As things arise, pay attention. Do you feel any sensations in your body? Has your awareness been brought to any physical pain, old injuries, or chronic physical struggles? Do you feel tightness in your chest, stomach, or forehead? This part might feel hard. That's okay. Sometimes the hardest part is just sitting with the discomfort. See if you can do it.

You may start thinking of all the ways you've behaved in the past to avoid uncomfortable thoughts or feelings instead of sitting quietly with them. There are many reasons for this. When we don't feel ready or capable to manage difficult thoughts, feelings, emotions, or sensations, we often reach for some kind of distraction. This is natural. But right now, resist that urge. Try to welcome the discomfort, and honor yourself for the bravery this takes.

Are you able to accept yourself and what you are experiencing right now? If so, this means you are on the path to healing. If the answer is no, don't worry—just put whatever came up back in its container, practice self-care, and come back to this exercise later to try again. And give yourself a hug—you just took an honest step inward.

Your Support Network

What does your current support network look like? Is it healthy? Is there a balance in which all parties feel safe and supported? Do you have a range of options in case one person isn't available at a time of need? Support can come in many forms, and it can change as necessary. Here are some common sources of support I recommend cultivating:

- *A trusted friend or family member*
- *A therapist*
- *A reiki therapist*
- *A practice of physical movement, such as yoga, dance, martial arts, running, or another athletic activity*
- *Soothing bath salts or essential oils*
- *An artistic outlet, such as writing, painting, or working with clay*
- *A relationship with nature*

There are also spiritual forms of support you can access if you feel so compelled. If this doesn't feel right to you, that's okay—go ahead and skip to the first self-care exercise on page 18.

Whatever you believe, spiritual beings are available and ready to assist you at all times. According to spiritual law, these beings cannot intervene with your free will. So, if you would like their support, you need to ask them specifically and give your permission. These beings take many forms, such as:

Archangels. It's believed that archangels are working behind-the-scenes to support the whole planet. It has been said that they can be in many places at once, and you are never bothering them when you ask for help, even for the smallest thing.

Guardian angels. It has been said that we are all born with at least one guardian angel. This angel is with you for your whole life, and available to you at all times.

Spirit animals. These guides may show up on your path in the form of real living animals, representations of animals in the form of images in your day-to-day life, or even as visions in your mind.

Spirit guides. Spirit guides are helpful beings that can come and go depending on our current life circumstances.

Spiritual figures. Depending on your beliefs, feel free to reach out to whatever figure you wish.

How do you ask for the help of your spirit team? In any way that's comfortable for you! Once you summon a spirit guide, you will know when they are with you; you will feel it in your being.

Listen to Yourself

A BIG PIECE of self-awareness is listening to yourself. This requires you to tune out outside voices and opinions (sometimes even those from your support network!) to listen to the voice of your true, knowing self.

The best way to do this is to get quiet and go within. The more you get to know yourself, the more you'll recognize the signs that you are doing something that you don't want to do or that doesn't align with your values. Listening to yourself leads to discernment—of which choice to make, which direction to go, and which person to trust. With the help of your support network and spiritual team, you can always find these answers within you.

On the other hand, we can have thoughts, reactions, or behaviors that we don't condone or believe in, but that just seem to come out of nowhere. This is natural. We are all human, and we are works in constant progress. It is important to acknowledge what comes up for you. When we keep our own thoughts and behaviors shadowed out of shame, it perpetuates a negative cycle and keeps us detached from ourselves.

However, the good news is, when you shed light upon your shadows, you can uncover your true motivations. Can you offer yourself some compassion and empathize with *why* you thought or acted the way you did in a given situation? Did you have a thought that came from a core belief or old pattern that no longer resonates with you? Did you lose control and act out of exhaustion or depletion? Once you can bring your shadows to the light, you gain the wisdom to know what you need in order to be truer to yourself next time.

BE PATIENT WITH YOURSELF

PATIENCE IS A form of compassion. And compassion for ourselves is key to self-acceptance. Being patient with ourselves throughout our life process—through the ups and downs and twists and turns, moments of confusion and moments of triumph—is one of the greatest gifts we can give ourselves.

It's simple but not easy. It takes time and effort, just like creating any new habit. Being patient with yourself means having empathy for wherever you are in your life journey. It means not judging yourself too harshly. It means remembering that it is not about how "far" you've come, but the strength it took to get to where you are.

You have a relationship with yourself, just like you have relationships with others. It takes time, compassion, and forgiveness to figure out what works for you. Prepare yourself for the work ahead by giving yourself the gift of patience.

In Her Own Words:
How You Got Here

The narrative of your life story is in your hands. No one can go back and change what's happened before this point, but we can review our story with patience and understanding. Reflecting on how we got where we are is an act of self-compassion. Understanding why we do what we do helps reclaim our personal empowerment to make changes going forward.

So, no matter what has occurred in your life story thus far, how you interpret your role will help clarify your inner strength. Within your viewpoint lies the freedom to embrace all aspects of your story and the wisdom to know that you control how it unfolds from here. With a clear understanding of your full self, you can rewrite your narrative from a place of empathy, growth, wisdom, and empowerment.

Here are some prompts to help you reflect on and reframe your story. Write your answers in your journal. Feel free to revisit this exercise for any situations in your past you'd like to examine more closely.

Can you remember a time when you were unhappy? Describe this time in detail. What were your external circumstances? How did you react or respond to them?

If you regret how you responded to the situation, take a moment to explore what might have caused you to react that way. Did the situation trigger past experiences or traumas? Did you have a positive role model during this time? Were you impacted by any stressors? Were you acting out of an emotional pattern rather than a place of empowerment?

With your new understanding of your motivations during this time, extend compassion to yourself and the possible reasons behind your actions. Note any good qualities you may have displayed during this time. Reframe any negative behaviors or reactions from a place of understanding.

Knowing yourself the way you do now, what would you have done differently? How do you think this different approach would have impacted your happiness or unhappiness, even if the circumstances remained the same? What was within your control?

Appreciate Yourself

LET'S REFLECT ON some qualities that you appreciate in yourself! Acknowledging and recognizing our positive qualities can help us reframe any harmful narratives we've been carrying inside.

For example, maybe you felt victimized in a specific situation. Take a moment to consider the positive qualities you brought to this situation. Kindness? Compassion? Empathy? Though you may have previously viewed something through the lens of victimization, you can refocus your story by recognizing your core qualities that carried light through the darkness.

Check off all the following qualities that apply to you (and feel free to add your own), and then pick your top three—those qualities you admire most. After you've chosen, go back to the story you explored in the previous exercise. Add these three qualities of yours to the narrative and reflect on how they may have served you in that situation.

※ Kindness	※ Discernment
※ Compassion	※ Wisdom
※ Empathy	※ Intuition
※ Courage	※ Fortitude
※ Thoughtfulness	※ Faith
※ Determination	※ Other _____

Which did you choose? These are your core qualities, that we'll explore more in depth in the next chapter.

Your Contributions Matter

DO YOU KNOW any women who regularly undervalue their achievements? Are you one of these women? From what I observe in my practice, this is all too common among women today. Women are balancing more than ever between career and home life, yet still have a tendency to downplay—or fail to be recognized or acknowledged for—these accomplishments.

Sadly, this has been true throughout history. Traditionally, "feminine" achievements have not been recognized for their true value, and are still often dismissed or discounted. How often do you see the feminine traits of kindness, nurturing, wisdom, caregiving, and quiet strength recognized as achievements in society? Not often enough. But it is this quiet, dedicated work that is the work of the goddess.

All of your achievements matter, no matter how much external recognition they do or do not receive. The personal feeling of accomplishment, satisfaction, and pride is what's important—holding this feeling close and letting it empower you. You can learn to acknowledge your achievements by recognizing how accomplished you feel on your path and using your gifts in the greatest way. You will be able to see the results of your work through your cocreations with the universe. You can look for signs from your spiritual team, too.

Goddess archetypes can help you elevate your sense of recognition. As Mary Faulkner says in her book *Women's Spirituality: Power and Grace*, "when we live in very limiting circumstances, the very poverty of that experience creates a deep hunger or longing, and an archetype emerges. This may very well be the impetus behind the rise of the Goddess archetype today."

Archetypes bring hope. Why do they inspire us? Simply put, stories of others breaking barriers, creating through artistry, and bringing their visions to life can ignite an inner fire that motivates us to strive toward our dreams. Witnessing some-one's ability to overcome obstacles with great feats of strength is empowering—even if it's a fictional superhero! We all carry divinity within us, and we all have access to divine qualities, especially through gratitude. Uncovering your personal arche-type will help you acknowledge your own strength and value your achievements, even if they go unseen by the outside world. This personal empowerment will keep fueling your fire until you feel at peace.

Archetypes emerge when we are ready for them. Yours is just waiting to be claimed, along with your crown of personal sovereignty, through which *you rule you*. Are you ready?

CHAPTER **TWO**

Take Inspiration from Your Goddess Archetype

Now it's time to call forth your inner divinity. In this chapter, we'll work together to help you identify your goddess archetype and explore your core qualities so you can begin to share your light with others. You'll learn about goddess spirituality and how it can empower you on your journey.

Goddess Spirituality

THROUGHOUT HISTORY, GODDESS archetypes have held sacred space for women to find sanctuary in divine feminine energy, and to share their gratitude for the gifts of Mother Nature. Many of the early conceptualizations of goddesses arose from the awe of water nurturing crops and bringing sustenance to the people of the lands. People would bless bodies of water, personifying its divinity in the form of a goddess with whom they could connect and interact. Goddesses also took the form of fire for divine warmth, and the form of an erupting volcano for anger and rage.

Divine feminine energy is receptive and about nurturing, giving, and having healthy boundaries. Anger is a natural emotion, and when recognized among divine beings, it helps justify the feeling itself and the importance of enforcing healthy boundaries. Fire is beautiful and should be honored and respected, like the divine spark within all of us. Elemental energy can be recognized in the form of earth and nature spirits. Feminine and masculine energy live harmoniously among the elemental kingdom, and divine feminine energy helps nurture that. Divine masculine energy helps protect it.

Rooted in feminism, goddess spirituality has been personified in the forms of goddesses, matriarchs, healers, and priestesses throughout time. It takes a different perspective than that of a patriarchal worldview.

Throughout history, goddess archetypes have been called to guide spiritual growth as well as larger social movements. Goddess spirituality summons forces such as love, beauty, strength, wisdom, mysticism, youth, connection, protection, sensuality, fertility, compassion, kindness, and fierceness.

When you identify the goddesses that align with your archetype and lived experiences, you can tap into divine feminine energy to guide your path toward your true light, self-acceptance, and self-care. Embracing the goddess means claiming the value of feminine traits and allowing yourself to be empowered by them.

That said, goddess spirituality does not mean holding up women as "better." We all have masculine and feminine energy within us and both are of value. Goddess spirituality means valuing the feminine as much as the masculine, which sadly has not been common practice through the centuries of human existence. Eastern cultures recognize the balance of masculine/feminine through *qi* energy and the duality of yin and yang. On a spiritual level, balancing your own personal yin (feminine) and yang (masculine) energy can help you feel the wholeness of your true self. On a societal level, this balance is important for a united collective experience.

THE THREE FACES OF THE GODDESS

ASPECTS OF FEMININE energy have been compared to the phases of the moon. Waxing, full, and waning stages represent cycles, gateways, and key passages of life. The three aspects—or faces—of the goddess are the maiden, mother, and matron.

Maiden. Waxing crescent moon. This represents youthful joy, playfulness, growth, innocence, creativity, exploration, and inner-child musings.

Mother. Full moon. This holds nurturing qualities for birth of all kinds, including ideas, projects, and transformation. It represents manifestation and responsibility.

Matron. Waning crescent moon. The matron energy carries spirituality and wisdom related to endings, death, and the cycle of life.

Note that the faces can apply to various life stages and experiences; they are not necessarily linear. Their application is inclusive to everyone who identifies as female, or even just one's inner feminine energy. In recent years, these archetypes have expanded to include not only stages of life, but also personal preferences and affinities. For example, some may seek out marriage and children (mother), others may prioritize career endeavors (matron), and others may place their focus on playful creativity (maiden). Any one or more of these faces can be present at any given time. Take strength and inspiration from the faces as they apply to you.

Feminine energy is in all of us, but the physical female body can vary depending on life stage as well as one's individual form. Female hormones are also affected by cycles within the reproductive system, and this also varies based on life stage as well as one's individual body. Reproductive organs may be in some female bodies, and not in others. We are not defined by our bodies, but we can take wisdom from the three faces of the goddess in a spiritual sense.

MAIDEN GODDESS ASTRAEA

Astraea, the star maiden of ancient Greece, is a virgin goddess of justice and innocence. The last of the immortals to live on earth, she stayed among the humans until the Iron Age. Her hopes for peace and harmony motivated her to stay as long as she did, but ultimately, she ascended to heaven to become the constellation of Virgo. Legend has it that she will one day return as herald for the utopian Golden Age that she represents.

WHAT'S YOUR GODDESS ARCHETYPE?

IT IS TIME to awaken to your inner divinity. Just as goddesses vary in their archetypes and individual qualities, so do humans. We are all born with different gifts, and you might be inspired to discover a goddess archetype already within you! Let's focus on your combination of qualities to see which divine gifts you have already mastered from your goddess archetype.

1. Someone gives you a bag of crystals. What do you do with them?

    A. Clean them with water or salt and charge them under the sun.
    B. Give them to your spiritual friend. Who needs crystals?
    C. Sage them and charge them under the moon.
    D. Analyze each crystal separately by consulting books and researching all their ancient uses.
    E. Follow A, C, and D, and start applying the crystals to healing remedies for all of your friends.

2. A new health food store opens up around the corner. What do you do?

    A. Go check it out and see if they carry your tried-and-true favorites.
    B. Head right over, introduce yourself to the staff, and do a big shop to stock up your pantry.
    C. Pop in to browse the aisles and check out the selection, dreaming up new dishes you might make in the future.
    D. Wait to check it out until you have a list of items and ingredients you really need.
    E. Buy some healthy products to share with a friend in need or a local shelter.

3. You feel an earthquake. What do you do?

    A. Take deep breaths. Center yourself.
    B. Run outside to see who you can help in your immediate area.
    C. Check in with your intuition before deciding your next move.
    D. Jump into your earthquake action plan, which you created months ago.
    E. Figure out who are the most vulnerable in the situation and find a way to help.

4. You win a spot to be a game show contestant. The first question you are asked is: *How do you best express yourself?* You answer:

    A. By sharing your new recipe ideas for healing foods with your friends.
    B. With hugs.
    C. Through mystical crystal intuitive artwork.
    D. By writing a blog post.
    E. By singing.

5. Good news: You won the game show! Now choose your prize:

    A. An Instant Pot.
    B. A rainbow.
    C. Your own art studio.
    D. The latest technology.
    E. A karaoke machine.

Mostly As: Spiritual from a grounded perspective.
You work with natural elements to nurture yourself and humanity. You are the person whom others seek out for comfort and rationality.

Mostly Bs: Guided by super strength.

You have developed all kinds of muscles through your life lessons. You are strong, decisive, and confident. You have worked hard to survive what has come your way, and people look to you for a helping hand.

Mostly Cs: Spiritual from a dreamy perspective.

Your creativity and intuition have been your guides since childhood. Though you may not always have trusted your gifts, people enjoy your works of art and are inspired by what you create.

Mostly Ds: Guided by intellectual empowerment.

You rely on empirical evidence. People turn to you for logic and security. You always seem to know just what to do and are the first to start working on practical solutions to a problem.

Mostly Es: Guided by heart-centered connectivity.

You are most happy when others are happy. You have boundless unconditional love. People rely on you and come to you when they need to talk and want to feel truly heard.

Write your results in your journal, and spend five minutes reflecting on how this goddess type resonates with you. Revisit your archetype often. It is always with you and can be summoned at any time.

Mother Goddess Asherah

Asherah, a Canaanite goddess, is recognized as a mother goddess, and her historical roots are among the trees. Her name has been translated to mean "grove," and her nurturing presence has often been depicted with sacred wood. In the company of her lion, she holds lilies and serpents in her hands. Associated with the tree of life, Asherah has been considered a gateway to divine wisdom.

See Your Inner Goddess

HAVE YOU STARTED to recognize your inner divinity?

As you develop a strong sense of your gifts and values, you can learn to tap into them to navigate any situation that comes your way. You'll know how to integrate what gives you joy into your grounded, human, perfectly imperfect existence.

Your goddess archetype might also help you connect with the divinity of others. As your spirit lifts, your energetic frequency will resonate with similar high vibrations within the universe. The light that shines through you will inspire the divine spark within others. You will begin to attract people and circumstances that match your higher vibration, taking your potential to new and unknown heights.

MATRON GODDESS
SPIDER GRANDMOTHER

The legend of Spider Grandmother has been passed down through myth from the Hopi Tribe. Appearing in stories throughout the Southwest, she is symbolized by her encompassing web. It is said that she manifested the world into existence through the web of her thoughts.

She is a leader, healer, and wise guide. Creator of the four directions, she is a protective force that helps people ascend. May the wisdom of Spider Grandmother guide us as we ascend to higher consciousness.

Your Core Qualities

YOUR DIVINE NATURE is always sacred and a source of inspiration. Everything that has happened to you, as well as all the healing you have done for yourself and others, is part of your divine nature.

Let's look at a couple of examples from the celestial realm.

In both mythology and astrology, Chiron (a centaur and also a comet) has been called the "Wounded Healer." He is a teacher known for his healing abilities but could not heal himself. He represents one's deepest wounds. Chiron was discovered in 1977 by Charles Kowal as the first astrological body of its kind, the centaur.

Connected to Chiron, Chariklo is a minor planet and centaur. Her more recent discovery in 1997 by James V. Scotti prompted astrologers Pam Gregory and Melanie Reinhart to speak of the healing properties of the small solar system body of Chariklo. They describe her as a receptive yin energy with a gift for creating or holding "sacred space" for transitions. Gregory and Reinhart have described Chariklo as returning to the collective consciousness at this time of great transformation. She is said to be here to assist in the ascension of planet Earth and her inhabitants. You can observe Chariklo's movements as she forms aspects with other planets, and you can connect to her healing energy.

Astrologer Heather Ensworth has spoken of Sedna—the dwarf planet that exists far from the sun and is named for the Inuit goddess of the sea—as a messenger. She feels that Sedna has come forth to alert us to a time of transition connected to collective repressed trauma and shadow elements.

As you can see, even the wounded have been immortalized in the night sky. Yet it is not their wounds that have defined them, but their journeys that shine bright and inspire awe and transformation. The same is true for you.

Let's reflect back upon the qualities that you embraced as your own in chapter 1 (page 20). In that exercise, you explored how those qualities empower and serve you, even in difficult situations. Now let's consider how they make up your divine goddess energy—your unique constellation of gifts that shine bright through the night sky to guide and heal others.

Compassion. Compassion is rooted in unconditional love. If you are a naturally compassionate person, you have an impressive capacity for love that sees far beyond the flaws in others. You know that humans are imperfect and yet worthy of deep love. You are able to love without expectation and are a role model for those around you.

Courage. You have physically or emotionally survived difficult situations, and these experiences lead you to live with an admirable fearlessness. Your courage invokes calm in those around you.

Determination. You have a strong will to get back up and try again. You are not easily deterred from your goals or tasks. You possess laser focus when something needs to be done, and this makes you an effective leader.

Discernment. You're able to sort through complex situations or challenges with relative ease. You have a strong sense about other people and form relationships wisely. When faced with a difficult choice, you know what to do and don't look back. Others are inspired by you to be more confident in life.

Empathy. You know how to let others have their own experiences without putting your expectations on their choices or actions. You understand that everyone is different and can easily put yourself in the shoes of others. This is a great gift for anyone who knows you.

Faith. You believe in miracles. You know there is a higher power at work. Your trust in the divine brings calm to you and those around you. Even when life is challenging, you always hold faith that things are just as they are supposed to be. You radiate light in darkness.

Fortitude. You are not a creature of comforts. You rise to any occasion and do what's needed without fanfare. Doing for others, even if it's something you do not want to do, comes naturally. In times of hardship, others are grateful to have you around.

Intuition. Your inner star shines brightly, guiding you in everything you do. Externally, you are a bright star for others who trust your guiding light.

Kindness. Think about the concepts of "paying it forward" and "random acts of kindness." If you are blessed with the innate gift of kindness, you are already helping others all the time. You are a bright light for anyone in your life.

Thoughtfulness. It's easy for you to act selflessly and give freely to others. You sometimes know what others need before they tell you. This leads to peace and harmony within your family or community. Others tend to have great appreciation for your thoughtful words or acts.

Wisdom. Others frequently come to you for advice, yet you are wise enough to know not to give advice unless explicitly asked for it. You have the ability to bring forth the wisdom in others as they make their own choices and decisions. You radiate energy of the Matron.

Take a moment to write in your journal about how your core qualities relate to your goddess archetype. Your divinity is emerging and taking form. This is who you are and who you always have been—let it surface!

DIVINE, BUT NOT PERFECT

AS YOU LEARN to embrace your goddess archetype and core qualities and share them with others, always remember that you are still human. Our inner divinity is meant to help us connect to our spiritual selves and higher power, not hold ourselves to an impossible standard. Connecting with divinity can provide comfort, courage, empowerment, and clarity. It can also provide the strength and humility needed to navigate life's challenges as an imperfect human.

It is important to translate these divine qualities into the human experience, and this takes self-awareness and self-compassion for your limits here on Earth. Working with your archetype and qualities can help you live as your authentic self.

IN HER OWN WORDS:
Let It Shine

Time to rise and shine!

I truly believe that our spiritual self is a pure ray of light emanating from our soul and illuminating our path ahead. Take a moment to close your eyes and envision your true light. Imagine that it fills you up, lighting up all parts of yourself, and radiates outward into the world. Think about all the ways you want this light to shine.

Now grab your journal. Write down the opening lyrics of the classic song "This Little Light of Mine":

This little light of mine
I'm gonna let it shine . . .

Then take five minutes to freewrite all the ways you will let your light shine in the world!

"This Little Light of Mine" was written as a children's song in the 1920s. It has since become an anthem for civil rights, personal freedoms, inner divinity, and shining one's light for uniting in peace. This song is taught in preschools and summer camps, where children sing out and shine bright from a place of divinity. It has also become an anthem for holiday festivals of light in celebration of miracles.

Honor the Journeys of Other Women

EMBODYING YOUR OWN divine spark helps you connect with the divinity of others. As you live in your true light, it's important to recognize this light in others. The more we lift each other up, the higher we will fly. Sadly, society has traditionally encouraged women to compete with each other, judge each other harshly, and even cut each other down. Goddess spirituality calls for the opposite of that. Each of us has our own unique authenticity. Collectively, that's one divinely blazing fire.

Feminine empowerment is sustainable only through connectedness, not competition. Sharing our light in no way diminishes our flame. All women are unique and special. Honoring each other creates the community that is vital to all of humanity.

Now that you have done the work to connect with yourself, with your goddess archetype and core qualities, and with other uniquely gifted women, it's time to deepen your relationship with yourself. The light you bring to the world can only be seen when it has been protected and cared for, and you are its caregiver.

CHAPTER **THREE**

YOUR RELATIONSHIP WITH YOURSELF

Now that you've actively taken steps toward embracing yourself and your gifts, let's tend to your divine spark. How is your relationship with yourself? Do you love yourself unconditionally? Do you recognize your value? Do you feel uncomfortable with any aspects of yourself? Are there behaviors you do not like? Are pieces of your soul hiding behind shadows, subconsciously distorting thoughts and behaviors? Shamans speak of fragmentations of the soul being split off through trauma. We all have the ability to call these pieces of the soul back to ourselves (and reach out for professional help with this if needed). In this chapter, we'll explore some tools for working on your most important relationship—the one with yourself—so you can bring your whole self to the light.

The Most Important Relationship

OUR RELATIONSHIP WITH ourselves is the foundation for all other relationships. When we are critical with ourselves, we tend to be more critical of others. When we are gentle with ourselves, we are gentle and more compassionate with others.

Our internal divine spark is also a magnet for connection. In order for this spark to shine through, it's necessary to embrace our full self.

Your spark has been with you all your life. The best way to reconnect with it is to think back to a moment of joy from your childhood. Even if it's just the smallest detail, can you think of a moment like this? Imagine being a kid and going on a Ferris wheel for the first time. Visualize waiting in a long line in the hot sun. When it's finally your turn, what does it feel like to finally sit down and buckle up? Feel the anticipation as everyone else gets on board. Now the wheel starts to move. It goes up and up, all the way to the top. You cannot believe how much you can see and how elevated you feel! Then it starts heading down back to the earth—can you feel a cool breeze? See the ground and all the people below. Align all of your senses with this moment. This kind of pure joy is your inner fire, your spark. You can find it, recognize it, and honor it at any time.

We have all been through some things that have dulled, dimmed, or even seemingly extinguished our spark. Maybe you don't even remember what your inner fire feels like. When you make room to honor your spark, it has the ability to warm you like the sun. And, it will light your way to the next best step. It will help you block out what does not honor you. You can learn how to protect your energy so no one can dampen your flame.

How you see and honor yourself signals to others how they can treat you. You deserve to be treated with kindness and respect—everyone does. To allow for your divine spark to shine through, you must create this foundation of honor and respect for yourself and protect it. This is an ongoing process that involves taking care of yourself, as well as respecting the divinity in others. Don't you feel better when you feel cared for? The most important person to care *for* you *is* you.

It is only natural to look to others for confirmation and support. In childhood, this was not only developmentally appropriate, but necessary for survival. Your experience of early attachment may inform how you treat yourself today. For instance, it might feel like second nature to derive self-worth and self-esteem from others; this can happen when your original source of love made value judgments about your choices or sent the message that their love was conditional. In moving forward, it is essential to become aware of any core wounding and start to maintain a healthy relationship with yourself. This relationship with self will become your foundation for all good things, including healthy relationships with others.

Though it can feel gratifying to receive "love" that you worked so hard to earn, you certainly don't need to become what someone else values in order to be deserving of love. You are worthy just as you are! Real self-worth comes from valuing yourself regardless of what others may think. No matter what you experience, your relationship with yourself is your solid safe haven, and should be cared for as such. It needs to be nurtured and protected, and you're the one to do it!

START REPAIRING YOUR RELATIONSHIP WITH YOURSELF

THE FIRST STEP toward repairing your foundational relationship with yourself is to sit quietly. This can be challenging, yet it is so important. In fact, it's one of the first things I do when working with a new client. It is within this stillness where you will be able to examine your connection to yourself and notice all the subconscious ways you talk to and treat yourself. This takes time and dedicated effort, but once you tap into a practice of quieting the external world so you can turn within, it will become easier and easier.

Let's take a moment to get quiet and reflect on your current relationship with yourself. Close your eyes and breathe deeply until your mind starts to settle. Once you feel centered, grab your journal and jot down answers to the following questions:

Do you treat yourself the way you treat friends and family members you care about?

If not, what's the difference?

Do you treat yourself the way you would like others to treat you?

If not, what's the difference?

Do you treat others the way you would like to be treated?

Can you identify any unhealthy relationship patterns that seem to keep repeating?

Spend a moment reflecting on your answers. What comes up for you? Identify three ways in which you could improve how you treat yourself, and make a commitment to work on them over the next week. Revisit these questions in a week, and see if and how your answers have changed. You can repeat this exercise weekly until you feel you've made some solid progress in how you relate to yourself.

MAKE TIME FOR THE MOST IMPORTANT RELATIONSHIP

SOMETIMES WE HAVE to create space to have time for ourselves—and create the time to have space for ourselves. It takes effort and conscious awareness to create this capsule for healing. And you are worth it. You deserve it, and your relationships with others deserve it.

Though it might seem counterintuitive, self-care is actually one of the least selfish things you can do. You require a certain amount of care. Think of this like fuel for a vehicle. The vehicle needs fuel in order to function. We all need to refuel our tanks to avoid feeling depleted and consequently "running on empty." If we try to run on empty, our performance in life will be poor. Our relationships will suffer. Our work will suffer. Our well-being will suffer.

Part of having a strong relationship with yourself is knowing how you refuel, and making time for it. This process looks different for everyone, as we all have different needs.

How do you refuel? Take out your journal and write down the first three to five things that come to mind. Vow to make space for all of them this week.

By taking charge of your own self-care, you will be empowered to show up as your best self in relationships with others. It all starts with your relationship with you.

EMBRACE YOUR SHADOWS

It can be challenging to master self-compassion, especially if there are parts of yourself that you are still learning to love. The only way through to the other side is to hear out the messages behind the shadows.

You can think of the shadow self as what has been sep-
arated from you—cut off. These are the parts of yourself
you are afraid to look at. We all have them. Do not be
afraid to see your shadows. Shadows are created from
wounds, likely in an attempt to feel safe. You can heal
these wounds by embracing them, which naturally brings
them into the light to transmute. Transmuting shadow
energies starts with bringing the shadow's subconscious
motivations into conscious awareness. Bringing shadows
into conscious awareness empowers you to transform
shadows into healthier thoughts, emotions, behaviors,
and spiritual energies.

When we don't listen to the messages deep within our
shadow self, the driving forces behind these messages
will continue to control our thoughts, behaviors, and
emotions. Get in the driver's seat by being brave enough
to take control of your own darkness. It is part of your
empowerment!

Invite these shadows into conscious awareness. When
safely held by empathy, defense mechanisms will reveal
themselves to you and start to dissolve. You can facilitate
this by speaking to yourself with kindness and compas-
sion (more on this in the next section). Shadow elements
exist for a reason: They are trying to protect you. When
you assert that you don't need their protection, that you
are strong and secure enough without them, they will
cease to exist.

When transmuting your shadows, you'll want to let
your emotions flow through you like water. Emotions
need to be seen and honored, and not judged, in order to
transform. Here are some examples of shadow elements
and how you might let them flow through you.

SHADOW: Rage.

LIGHT: I see your anger. *Is there hurt underneath it? Was your voice not heard or honored the first time you spoke up? Did you become angry and still yielded no positive results? Did frustration escalate your anger to rage, and now your behaviors feel out of your control, as they are driven by this shadow motivation? Go back to the part where you felt hurt. You have a right to all your feelings, and you are allowed to feel hurt. It doesn't feel good to not be seen or not have your feelings honored; I can see why you would be angry. Use your voice and speak up. Enforce healthy boundaries if necessary and protect your energy by giving yourself the love and validation you seek. Empower yourself by transmuting the fire of your rage into a directed spark of assertion.*

SHADOW: Destructive behaviors.

LIGHT: Do you feel sad? Do you feel like there is no way out of that sadness? Does it seem like you are in an endless black hole spiraling down into hopelessness? Sadness is a very natural part of the human experience. *It can be very frustrating to feel sad and lose hope. When it feels like you cannot see the light, destructive behaviors may manifest out of anger, frustration, or feelings of unfairness. It may be an attempt to take control of a situation that feels out of control. Acknowledge all these feelings to return to your center of strength within. Regain your sense of control by reaching out to your higher power (it should feel light and positive), connect with a therapist, or seek professional care to help with medicinal options.*

SHADOW: Suffering.

LIGHT: There is a Buddhist saying that pain is inevitable, but suffering is a choice. *Accept that you are in pain, and that it is for a reason. Remove any layers of guilt or shame, move toward taking responsibility only for what is your responsibility, and allow yourself to focus on healing. We will all experience pain in this lifetime. It is part of our human and spiritual process, maybe even part of our soul growth. You do not need to rush your process, but you also do not need to suffer extensively. Give yourself permission to keep the soul growth, release your suffering, and do the healthy things you need to do to honor your pain.*

SHADOW: Attempting to control others.

LIGHT: Has your inner child experienced deep wounding? Do you fear that your emotions and feelings of safety and security are subject to the actions of others? Sometimes we turn the tables in an attempt to prevent a familiar painful situation or relationship dynamic. *Fear of abandonment can take many forms, but often it triggers doing something to someone else before they can do it to us. While it is empowering to take control of our own self, it is not necessary or healthy to attempt to control another person. We are all on our own paths, and the best thing we can do is heal our own inner child and then set healthy boundaries. Honor your inner child by taking your concerns seriously, and then doing the work to heal. You can manage these shadows safely when they are in your awareness and your focus is on creating healthy relationships.*

In your journal, identify three shadows that live in the dark side of your moon, and then flow them into the light to channel your divine gifts.

We'll do more shadow work in the next chapter.

How You Talk to Yourself

BEING KIND TO yourself creates a safe space for any fearful parts of yourself to emerge and heal. The first step in being kind to yourself is changing how you talk to yourself.

What is self-talk? It's how we speak to ourselves internally. You know that voice that's constantly talking in your head, narrating your experiences and interactions as you go about your day? In fact, this voice is so constant that at times you might not even realize it's there. Take a moment to tune into your voice. Reflect on the following:

How do you talk to yourself?

What story are you telling?

What's the tone? The overall approach?

Do you often hear this voice criticizing you?

What are common themes from this voice?

Do the words, tone, or intent feel familiar to you? Do they echo a relative or someone involved in your early attachment?

When you recognize your inner divinity, you will see that how you talk to yourself is also how you talk to the universe! "Valence" is a term used in psychology to describe a positive or negative affect placed upon something. In this context, the valence you give your self-talk affects the energy of your words—and what you attract in life will tend to match this energy. For example, even if you tell yourself "I want this," if the undertone is a fear that you don't deserve it, the universe will match that negative valence—the energy of you not having it—and you likely won't get the outcome you're after. The universe and your inner divinity are listening carefully and will respond to the vibrational frequency you send yourself.

Negative self-talk undermines your sense of self-worth and potential. Some examples of negative self-talk are thoughts like:

You're not going to be able to do all that today.

You're going to fail.

Everyone at work is more productive than you.

You haven't been a good enough parent.

You will never be able to do what that person is doing.

If you feel like you engage in negative self-talk, please don't feel shame about it. It is a perfectly human response to our conditioning and environment. The work is to practice becoming aware of it happening, and then redirect it with compassion.

For example, if you wake up telling yourself, "I'll never get it all done today," stop and pause. Reframe the thought into something compassionate and positive, such as: "Today I am going to make the most of my circumstances. I am going to do as much as I can and believe in myself. I am a beautiful soul and I am ready to work toward my goals. I would rather give it my best shot than not try at all."

You owe it to your divine self to treat yourself with utmost compassion. You only have this one life as you. Unlived potential is a shadow by itself. I invite you to step out of the shadows.

Let's explore the way you speak to yourself a little more deeply. Think of something that happened recently that you considered to be a "mistake." By "mistake," I mean even the slightest thing you may feel you did wrong. Now write down a statement you heard in your head, a judgment you may have felt in your heart, or words you may have said to another person after this happened.

Can you define the origin of these words or thoughts? Did these thoughts, statements, judgments, or emotions come from a relationship you've had in the past or have currently? You have the power to create your own self-talk. The first step is to actively release old patterns and thought loops. It will be like creating a new habit, and therefore, it will take time. You are creating new neural pathways in your brain. These will have to be practiced repeatedly, but over time they will become second nature.

It's so much easier to default to a well-known and well-worn path, especially when you are not consciously paying attention, or when you are feeling overwhelmed or depleted. That is why it is so essential to hold the time and space for yourself to practice self-care.

RETHINKING SELF-TALK

HERE ARE SOME examples of common negative sentiments, and suggestions for positive reframing.

Instead of saying	Try saying
I failed.	I tried my hardest and will find the strength to keep trying. I am human, and this is a process. I will recalibrate and ensure that my goals are manageable.
I knew this would happen. I always do this.	It takes time and compassion to create new healthy habits. It is a perfectly imperfect process filled with trial and error. I will celebrate every milestone, even if it feels like one step forward and two steps back. I will reward myself for taking the step at all. I will honor the new muscles I am building in the process.
Why do I even bother trying? I just want to give up.	I give myself permission to take a break. I will listen to my body wisdom. I listen to my soul wisdom. I will find a safe space, keep myself safe, and take the time I need before I continue.

SPEAK POSITIVELY

HOW WE SPEAK to ourselves creates an energetic vibration. Words themselves hold vibrational frequencies, and you contain the energy of how you speak to yourself. Now that you're familiar with some of your internal scripts, here are a few simple ways to rewrite your script and start speaking more positively to yourself. Give each one a try and find which works best for you. Remember, positive self-talk is a habit, so pick one or two of these and commit to trying them consistently for the next few weeks. It may be hard at first, but it will get easier!

* Think about your ideal relationship. How do the partners treat each other? How do they speak to each other? Now start practicing your ideal relationship by interacting in this way with yourself.
* Now that you're skilled at identifying negative self-talk, whenever you have a negative thought about yourself or your behavior, come back to the idea that life is an imperfect process for everyone, and that you are moving forward.
* Take the previous tip a step further. When a negative thought arises, remember that we are all facing our own internal struggles. Then, create and hold the space to transmute shadows into light with your newly revised self-talk. Sit with the discomforting thought and embrace it for just a moment. You are creating the containment necessary to transmute negative energy. As you gently listen to this thought, and "hear it out," have compassion for the source within you that has allowed for such a thought to exist. Now that you've accepted the thought, give yourself permission to feel safe without this negative thought. How does that feel?
* The next time a negative thought arises, remind yourself that this is a challenging but rewarding process, and it takes practice and time. You are starting just by making the effort to try. Remember: True progress is made with manageable goals. It is important to progress at *your own pace.*
* Motivational interviewing is a questioning technique used by therapists to meet a client in a difficult process and help guide them through ambivalence. For example, someone

may have the intention and desire to make a change, but get stuck when it comes to taking the first step toward the change. The idea is to work together at the point of ambivalence, helping the client come to an understanding of what is necessary to take that step. You can try this with yourself. First, acknowledge where you are in your process and where you might be getting stuck. This is valuable information. Sit with the stuck feeling in a space of compassion to understand it better. Ask it, why are you there? Why are you stuck? Do any responses that come up for you feel familiar or similar to an old pattern? Where does this pattern originate? Honor why the feeling stayed stuck in an attempt to protect you. Make sure you acknowledge to yourself that there is no judgment. Do you still need it to protect you? Are you afraid to take the next step? Can you actively name what you would need to feel safe enough to release your defense mechanisms? Can you give yourself what you need to feel emotionally safe enough to move forward? Ask yourself what you need in order to release the stuck emotion or defense. There is always a reason why something is stuck, and your emotions are always valid. Embrace your emotions to begin healing, and let them flow through you to release them. You can even thank them for doing their job and feel closure in telling them goodbye.

※ Practice speaking to yourself with pure, unconditional love and empathy. Use the same tenderness you would for a baby, a puppy, or your very best friend. You may start by just trying to figure out for yourself what words to use and how it would feel to hear them. It might be emotional to hear them. Keep trying. Let the emotions come. Honor this process. You are worthy.

The Goddess Tara

The goddess Tara is known from Hinduism and Tibetan Buddhism. Like Aphrodite, she was born from the water. Her name means "star," and she represents time. A bodhisattva (Buddha-to-be), she is the goddess of self-mastery and mysticism. She has been represented by both the fully opened lotus flower to symbolize day, and the half-opened lotus to symbolize night. The names "White Tara" and "Green Tara," respectively, reflect these two aspects of her majesty.

Through her variations, she holds aspects of divine compassion and protection through spiritual growth. Connected to day and night, she symbolizes embracing one's own inner shadows and light.

How You Think about Yourself

IN WHAT LIGHT do you see yourself? Do you often compare yourself to others? Do you hold others on a pedestal? Do you assume that others perceive you in a negative light?

While it is essentially impossible to see yourself objectively, it is important to see yourself in a compassionate light. Self-talk is one piece of the self-love puzzle. But how you perceive yourself as a whole is even more important. Even if you tell yourself positive statements, if you perceive yourself as less than or as unworthy, then true self-love won't be possible.

Self-love involves listening to yourself, treating yourself kindly, and having compassionate accountability for your behaviors. The way you perceive yourself is reflected back to you from the universe. This does not mean everything happens because of you—we don't have that type of control! But if you consistently feel low vibrational frequency emotions toward yourself (such as fear, apathy, guilt, and shame), what you get back from the universe will vibrate at a similar decreased vibration. This is often why we find ourselves stuck in many aspects of life during the periods when we don't feel good about ourselves. When you treat yourself kindly and believe you are worthy of healthy relationships, it sets a precedent for what you will allow into your life.

With self-compassion, you will gain the clarity and strength to connect with and trust your intuition and divine source. You are only in charge of you. Start by becoming your own best friend. It will make a world of difference—you'll see!

In Her Own Words:
Picturing Your Goddess

Let's go to dreamland with Neptune, planetary ruler of the spiritual realm and watery fantasy. Get your journal and pen ready for a fun journey. I also recommend lighting some candles or diffusing some essential oils to help awaken your senses.

Option 1: Freewrite your life story from the very beginning. It can be anywhere from 1 page to 20. Write yourself as a heroine who has survived and explain all that you have survived. Your true self is the light behind what it took to survive. Envision that pure light and say hello to your inner divinity.

Option 2: Picture (or invent) your goddess. You can choose an already-known goddess from a book, historical source, or classic artwork. Or, dream one up from your imagination—give yourself permission to drift off in this moment and see what comes to your mind's eye. When you've chosen your goddess, write her name in your journal. Sketch her form. Then list what inspires you about this character. Strength? Fortitude? Intelligence? Fertility? Lovability? Abundance? Write them down here.

Affirm Yourself

POSITIVE AFFIRMATIONS ARE powerful tools on the journey to self-love. When we affirm ourselves, we take control of our narrative. We are being assertive in creating the life we want.

Affirmations only work if they feel true to you. Your affirmations should organically originate from your true essence. As you think about affirmations for yourself, consider and journal the following:

What would you like to invite into your life?

What vibrations do you want your cellular structures to hold? Love, abundance, health? Something else?

What positive traits of yours do you want to keep front of mind?

Affirm to yourself what you would like to receive.

Here are some examples of my favorite personal affirmations:

- I am love.
- I hold divinity within myself.
- I have done the best I can with the tools I have had to work with at any given time.
- I am light.
- I can try again.
- I understand that self-compassion is an essential foundation for relationships with myself and others.

I am worthy of empathy.

I empathize with others and try to understand why they might do what they do.

I am my own best friend.

I hold healthy boundaries for myself.

I keep myself safe.

I hold myself accountable for my actions and behaviors.

I treat others how I wish to be treated.

I protect and honor my energy.

I am worthy of love.

IN HER OWN WORDS:
Affirmations

Let us willingly enter the darkness to welcome the affirmations from our personal spark:

Picture yourself at the bottom of a very deep and dark empty stone well. Someone from above throws you a rope. It is made of light and words. What are the words that give you the hope to ascend? These come from your soul. Freewrite them in your journal without overthinking it. Affirm your inner spark with these words.

Make Yourself a Priority

WHEN YOU KNOW that you matter, this energy is reflected in how others receive your energy.

Change starts with you. You are your top priority. If others are dependent on you, then it is even more important that you give yourself the gift of self-care and self-love. It is the only way you can show up in the world and for others from your spiritual self.

Addressing your own needs head-on (after welcoming them with self-compassion) will save you time, effort, and heartache. It will help connect you to your divine gifts and intuition, aligning you with an easier flow of life. You will not need to resist what you know you can handle. You will not find yourself stuck when you meet a crossroads.

Prioritizing yourself means treating yourself kindly, redirecting negative self-talk, respecting your own boundaries, and perceiving yourself as worthy of love, health, and happiness. Be generous with yourself during this process. Embrace any setbacks and keep going at your own speed. Soon you will learn to operate straight from your true inner strength: the strength that comes from prioritizing yourself and letting your soul shine its divine light that leads you out of darkness.

CHAPTER **FOUR**

Channel Your Divine Gifts

Goddesses exemplify many divine gifts. They are beautiful, each with unique constellations of special abilities. When you stop to think about it, you'll likely notice a thread of your special abilities woven throughout your lifetime. What is it that has carried you, motivated you, helped you get up when you thought you might not be able to face another moment of something difficult? What is your inspiration for living? What is your light through darkness?

Everyone Has Gifts

A DIVINE GIFT may be interpreted as something that comes very naturally to you and benefits the world around you. Such gifts are quite special. Some people believe these gifts are part of your soul and that, in fact, you may have fine-tuned these through many lifetimes!

For instance, do you have a talent for singing, dancing, or painting? It has been said that such artistic talent comes from a higher plane of existence. If you are naturally gifted in these areas, you may have the divine gift of inspiration. By embracing your gift, you inspire those who recognize the beauty of your artistry.

Do you have an innovative mind that lends itself to invention, scientific theories, or medicinal cures? This gift may be connected to special access to a field of consciousness where such ideas exist, waiting to be discovered. If you have this divine gift, you may be able to receive many gifts for humanity.

Do you have a gift for building, engineering, or math? Working toward practical solutions to increase others' comfort takes the divine gift of understanding the nature of the universe. If you have this divine gift, you help sustain the existence of life itself on Earth.

We all have our divine gifts. Part of the excitement is in discovering what yours might be.

It has been said that we are spiritual beings having a human experience. It might inspire you to know that the human body is made from stardust. In fact, we have about 97 percent of the same kind of atoms as our galaxy. Sometimes we have a hard time trusting our inner spark—our stardust—because we feel alone, isolated, or misunderstood. It is precisely at these times when it can help to go deep within and look at our divine gifts.

You were born with gifts specific to you, which is why your beauty is in your unique self.

Perhaps we all have different gifts so that we can connect. The divine spark in you can recognize the divine spark in another person. How do you feel when you hear a beautiful song? What rises from within you when a piece of art speaks to your soul? These are connections of divinity.

Divine gifts are channeled through your creations. What mediums calm you? Paint, words, elements of nature, human connection? Do you have an artist's soul? Are you nurturing to animals? Do others come to you for advice and support? Are you an intellectual, a visionary, a designer? When you create, you tap into your intuition and your divinity. Of course, since we live in a world of duality, these gifts can be used for light or dark. However, all the energy you put out will come back to you, so create wisely.

FOCUS ON YOUR STRENGTHS

WE ALL HAVE our strengths. Is there anything that has always come very naturally to you?

I will continue to remind you not to compare yourself and your skills to anyone else, ever. Your talents and strengths are yours alone to cultivate and develop. Besides, the world would be a boring place if we were all exactly the same.

Even the idea of having a "weakness" can feel painful. But often a weakness can give you a hint to the positive attribute it supports. For example, maybe group social interaction drains you, but you're an excellent listener one-on-one. You may feel drained because of the very gift that enables you to pay close attention. While this may feel like a weakness in one situation, it is a great strength in another. When you are able to recognize what makes you an individual, you can take ownership of your full self.

Shadow Work

SHADOWS ARE CONVENTIONALLY seen as the negative side of a personality—they're the things we prefer to ignore. Shadow work focuses on these hidden elements, asking you to explore your own core wounding. Why is this important? For one, you can get to know yourself more completely. Delving into this side of your personality also helps you see yourself and others with more clarity. With greater self-awareness, you can develop a pathway to personal development and self-compassion.

Strengths flourish in the light. Yet, sometimes they are shadowed by darkness. Your shadows are nothing but unembraced aspects of the self. If you take a shadow element and process its associated emotions with compassion, it is like you are warming it with the sun. It is only a shadow element because it is covered in shame, cut off, and buried. When one of these elements emerges, usually unexpectedly or out of your control, it's like an untamed dragon bursting from its cave.

Imagine an angry dragon. This dragon was born with wings, full of fire, and ready to fly. This dragon faced rejection early in her life, because people did not understand her. When this dragon lived in her shadows, she feared rejection. If someone approached her, she would breathe fire and fly away to defend against her worst fears.

Now imagine this same dragon has faced her shadows. Confidence radiates from her inner fire, as she can now consciously channel her power, instead of being driven by her subconscious motivations. She breathes a fiery assertion when necessary, and her wings carry her to majestic heights.

In his book *Psychology and Alchemy*, Carl Jung speaks of rites of renewal as "attempts to abolish the separation between the conscious mind and the unconscious, the real source of life, and to bring about a reunion of the individual with the native soil of his inherited, instinctive make-up."

Here, we will create our own rites of renewal. When greeting your shadows, remember that your top priority is to feel safe and supported. Keep your safe-space container imagery in your mind (see page 14) to stay in the perspective of the detached observer.

RITES OF RENEWAL

FOR THIS EXERCISE, we are going to welcome Sekhmet, the warrior goddess and goddess of healing. Depicted as a lioness, she has been called "Flaming One." Tap into your own self-compassion and affirmative self-talk to welcome your shadow qualities to arise within your consciousness. There is a reason they hide.

Sekhmet, the sun goddess of Egypt, has the head of a lion and wears a sun disk. As the meaning of her name reflects, she is powerful! Represented by the hottest heat of the sun, stories have been told of her fury. She was created as a weapon to destroy humans for their disobedience, and her wrath becomes incited by humanity. With her great power also comes an ability to heal, help humans avert plagues, and cure diseases. She was known to support physicians and healers and was believed to have a cure for every problem.

She is associated with the goddess Bast, who originated in the Nile Delta. It has been said that Bast is a tamer version of her former self. In this state, she visits as the household protector and cat goddess Bastet. While Bast brings physical and mental healing with the sun's nurturing rays, the lioness could bring drought and destruction. We all get angry—and we all have the power to heal.

What are your wings of fire? If you have ever hit rock bottom, you will know that something deep within you lit an inner fire to rise again. What was that inner fire? Can you name it? Get ready to break free.

Claim your wings. Here are some examples of wings of fire. Feel free to write your own in your journal depending on what comes up for you:

- Persistence to fulfill your life purpose
- Love for and dedication to others
- Belief in what you are trying to create
- Inner intuitive compass leading you on the path toward your inspiration
- Inner resolve and strong will to live and thrive

Shadow elements come from primal needs. When we don't learn healthy ways to meet our needs, unhealthy behaviors arise in response to feed the hunger. The more depleted we feel, the fewer resources we have to manage these impulses in healthy ways. When you are able to embrace your whole self, you can better understand your instincts and proactively feed them in a healthy way. Here are some examples of common shadows and their corresponding needs:

- **Shadow:** Hunger for power / **Need:** A sense of security
- **Shadow:** Unhealthy or harmful acts to prove self-worth / **Need:** Ego validation
- **Shadow:** Rage / **Need:** A way to release deep pain
- **Shadow:** Defensiveness / **Need:** Ability to see the truth and validity of one's own needs
- **Shadow:** Aggression / **Need:** To know that one's needs deserve to be met

Now take a moment to claim your needs and their corresponding shadows. In your journal, write down any that come up for you. As you do so, tell yourself right now that your needs are valid and there for a reason. When you remove layers of shame and guilt, you can bring your needs to light and act with assertion and confidence, rather than shadow habits. Feeding your instinctual needs in a healthy way prevents them from hungering badly enough to drive shadow behaviors.

When you care for your needs, you gain control of your own empowerment. You get to consciously decide where to go, instead of being controlled by shadows.

Shadow Gifts

Some of your strengths and talents may be shadowed right now. Let's go deep within and remember your gifts. Which of these shadows seem most familiar to you?

SHADOW: *You are overwhelmed by the energy of others, and this can sometimes lead to impulsive reactions. You sometimes feel emotions, seemingly out of the blue, and cannot understand what caused these feelings.*

NEED: *You need time alone to recover or process information at a very deep level.*

GIFT: *You might be an empath or highly sensitive person (HSP). An empath is someone who can feel other people's feelings with their heightened intuition. An HSP is someone who is acutely aware of external stimuli on a sensory level. Your gift is feeling energy. When you learn how to understand the feelings that come your way from* others as powerful messages, you can become an energy alchemist. With practice, instead of absorbing the energy of other people and situations, you can turn intuitions into important messages that bring light within yourself and to others. The ability to recognize and name these emotions is a beginning point for working with spiritual energy toward a place of peace and harmony for all.

SHADOW: *You have a strong voice and state your opinions boldly, sometimes offending others.*

NEED: *To be heard, understood, and validated.*

GIFT: *You are a gifted leader. When you can transmute your shadow, you'll understand that true leadership is not about talking the loudest or engaging in a power play, but in confidently speaking powerful truths that better the greater good.*

SHADOW: *You have chosen to be a caregiver, either professionally or as a role you take for friends and family. (This is different from being placed in this circumstance or pressured into this choice.) You feel depleted because you are taking care of so much and so many, and this can result in you not acting in your highest good.*

NEED: *To be helpful and seen as helpful.*

GIFT: *You are a caregiver. It is essential for you to learn and enforce healthy boundaries for self-care. Your gift is in nurturing others and Mother Earth, and holding divine feminine energy. You may find that you have a strong connection to your intuition and can communicate effectively with those who have trouble communicating. Honor this beautiful gift and prioritize self-care. The world desperately needs you now.*

SHADOW: *You love darkness. Things others might find disturbing, like death or gothic art, intrigue you. (P.S. The loving of darkness is actually light, because love is love!)*

NEED: *To see things for how they are, including the darker sides of life and cycle of life and death.*

GIFT: *You are a blessed shadow worker. The world needs you because you are not afraid. You are brave enough to go into the shadows, and you are comfortable working with this energy. You are able to embrace darkness itself, and understand that it is just as important as the light.*

SHADOW: *You struggle with money and always feel like you're living from a place of scarcity. This makes it difficult to thrive, and as a result you may fall into unhelpful survival mechanisms.*

NEED: *To be valued for more than monetary and material gains. To have others understand the value of art and creation above all else.*

GIFT: *You are the artist, poet, writer . . . Without the artist souls of this world, what would this world be? Your approach to the world is the very inspiration that gives hope, meaning, and motivation to our lives. Just because our current society doesn't always reward such inspiration with material gains doesn't undermine its value in any way. By honoring divine feminine energy on Earth, hopefully we will evolve into a system that gives greater respect to receptive yin qualities, such as creation, as well as intuition, kindness, and caregiving.*

Putting Your Gifts into Action

AS YOU GET more in touch with your gifts and your shadow self, you can begin a deeper, more holistic level of healing. This will help you feel more expansive and abundant. It will also raise your energetic frequency to manifest positive results.

Now that you're more familiar with your gifts, think about ways to put them into action. Recognizing and using your gifts will help you connect more deeply with yourself and others.

How would you like to channel your divinity? You can start small. Here are some journaling prompts to help.

What divine gift do you recognize in yourself?

In what healthy ways can you transmute and channel the shadow side of this gift?

What are three small things you can do this week to share your gift with the world?

This is a process, a buildup of using and sharing your gifts. And the nice thing about starting small is that you can start right now!

Spiritual Gifts

We all have spiritual gifts, and some are just being developed. In ancient times, high priestesses were considered essential to society. Their abilities to connect with Mother Nature enabled them to read energy and heal others. See if any of these gifts of the goddess resonate with you:

Do you like to decorate your home with crystals and natural materials because you think they look nice? You may find them visually appealing because you have connected with them on a deep level. This might mean you are a naturally gifted energy healer.

Are strangers drawn to you? Do people often open up and share their stories with you? You may be a naturally gifted therapist or life coach.

Are you botanically gifted? Aromatherapy, flower essences, and herbal remedies are fine healing arts. The ability to create medicinal substances may be a gift deep within you, passed down through your family line. With the proper credentials, you can offer the world your healing gifts.

Have you found your balance within? Do you enjoy helping others find and maintain their life balance? Your perspective on life could benefit others. You might be a spiritual teacher!

Do people marvel at your wisdom? Do you feel connected to ancient civilizations and find yourself wanting to know more? Open yourself up to receive your spiritual gifts, and let your intuition guide you to the line of work that calls you. Whatever job you do, your light will shine.

GET CREATIVE

CREATIVITY TAPS INTO your sacral chakra. It is an essential part of your rainbow bridge of chakras (see page 158), connecting you to your spiritual self and Mother Earth. Remember that creative gifts are not limited to artistic talent. Creativity includes self-expression of all kinds! Here are some beautiful forms of creativity you might recognize from your own life:

* Organizing a fun event
* Cooking a favorite meal
* The clothes, jewelry, makeup, or hairstyles you choose to wear
* The unique ways you connect with others to celebrate and understand them
* How you solve life's problems
* How and when you say no
* How you communicate with people
* Decorating your home

The sacral chakra energy center is also where the womb and female reproductive organs are located. This is the female center for creation itself (and is also true for nonbiological women or women who no longer have or never had these organs). Dreams of pregnancy can actually signify an idea coming to fruition that is ready to be born. There have been depictions of the goddess of creation as pregnant with the world! Can you relate?

Express your divine gifts by exercising your creativity. Take a class, join a group, or practice art, music, or dance. Whenever you explore something that inspires you creatively, it's like stretching your soul!

In Her Own Words:
Tree of Life

The tree of life is a concept that shows up in many religions. In the Abrahamic faiths, the tree of life appears in the Garden of Eden. What does your Garden of Eden look like? Create it! Fill your imagination with whatever nurtures you. Visualize your tree of life nurturing your spiritual self. In your journal, write or draw everything you wish to create in this world on the branches of your tree. What flowers will bloom when the sun shines upon your garden? Watch your tree stand strong as your roots grow deep into the flow of Earth's nutrients.

SHARE YOUR GIFTS WITH OTHERS

AS WE ARE all unique yet interconnected, collaborating with others is a powerful representation of our feminine strength.

In times of crisis, we are often moved by how people come together to connect and offer to help in any way they can. Creative and divine gifts are a big part of this. For example, in the 1980s, people expressed their love by submitting panels they created for the famous AIDS quilt, which were then stitched together into a collective expression of love and support. This quilt gained national attention as a representation of the human need to connect and heal each other. Such beautiful, creative acts of kindness and solidarity are born of the divine feminine and reinforce our interconnectedness. But we don't need crisis to bring us together—you can find the love within you to start creating with connection right now!

How will you share your gifts with others?

Now that you have seen yourself in the light of your strength, stardust, and divinity, it's time to identify what you most desire as the abundant fruits of your labor.

PART **TWO**

WHAT YOU WANT

The moon receives its light from the sun and reflects it through the darkness of night. This receptive quality is a divine feminine gift. Spiritually, when you are able to receive light in the darkness, you can sense beyond what comes through your five physical senses. You receive with your intuition, and the light of this wisdom can be reflected to guide your way. Now it's time to glow with the moonlight as we explore your intuitive gifts.

CHAPTER FIVE

GET IN TOUCH WITH THE WORLD AROUND YOU

From a strong foundational relationship with yourself, let's move into exploring your relationship with others and the world around you. This can help you clarify your purpose. We all have important roles to play. Fulfillment comes from being true to ourselves while also sharing our gifts. When you are in alignment with your spiritual self and inner divinity, your role will come naturally and be positively embraced by the universe. It will take some work to get to this healthy space, with healthy boundaries intact. But once you're there, you'll flourish. Let's get to work!

Get Outside of Yourself

GETTING OUTSIDE OF yourself means getting out of your own way. When you get too deep into your head, you can become lost and even forget your sense of purpose. Can you relate? The best way to break out of this space is to follow your heart to connect and collaborate with your community. This helps awaken capabilities you may not have realized you had, and can help you figure out how you fit into the world. Exploring your ties to humanity and the universe will help you further clarify your sense of self.

It can be tough to take that first step and engage with others. It requires vulnerability and courage. Fear of rejection or judgment may seek to hold you back, but it's important to push through these fears. Remember that all humans are on their own journey, working on their own insecurities and their own challenges with giving and receiving unconditional love. As you interact with others, let empathy be your best friend, and try not to take the perceived reactions of others too personally. By empathizing with yourself and others, you help bring authentic connection to light. It's the best step out!

Let's try an exercise. Take a deep breath. Imagine opening your front door to step out into the world and your community. Pay very close attention to all the thoughts and feelings that arise within you in that moment. Do any of them feel similar to the negative self-talk we worked on earlier? If so, write them down in your journal, and acknowledge them for trying to be of service. Now kindly say goodbye to them, and replace them with some positive self-talk. This is also a good time to recite your positive affirmations from the exercise on page 55.

Believe it or not, universal support is accessible to you at all times; you just have to be receptive to it. The universe may have been trying to reach you for quite some time; now is your chance to open the door to receive its offerings! As you open yourself up to others, keep your vibration high. You have already done this with your affirmations and positive self-talk. Faith, hope, and gratitude will also keep your vibration high during this process. If you need some extra support, go ahead and ask your spirit team for a sign. This can come in many forms, such as a feather, a coin, an image on a sign or a book cover, a phrase you hear on the radio or said by someone walking by.

To help you feel protected, you can visualize an energetic bubble around yourself, and infuse it with whatever you like. For example, you can visualize the words of a prayer, or the energy of a guardian angel. You can choose a color that helps you feel safe and imagine the protective energy as that color. Gemstones and crystals all have different properties, and you can carry your favorites for the type of support you would like on any given day. A meditation that sets your intention for the day can help you feel at peace, and you can even invite your spirit team along for guidance.

Getting outside yourself will give you important clues as to where you fit in the universe. Remember, your core qualities and divine gifts are only recognizable when they are embodied through human expression!

REFLECTIVE DISTANCE FOR YOUR SPIRIT

TAKE A DEEP breath! Taking deep breaths invites the outside world in and activates your spirit. When you get some distance from what's going on inside by getting in touch with the world around you, it is quite literally a breath of fresh air!

When you go outside to receive the bounty of nature, this experience opens and cleanses your heart chakra. The smells of flowers, grass, and trees can awaken primal senses of strength and survival. Soothing sights of nature may inspire your creativity and calm your adrenal system. The sounds of nature may resonate with vibrations in your being, connecting you to all of life and creation. The feel of the earth beneath your feet can ground you into your sense of purpose and belonging. Getting into balance with nature can calm your mind and body, allowing you to relax into a flow with the universe. This flow comes from connecting your conscious and subconscious mind so they may function in harmony. Energetically, this is a way to balance your inner feminine and masculine forces.

Can you think of a time when you were working on something and felt like you could not come up with the solution to a problem? Sometimes a change of pace and scenery is just what we need to activate different aspects of our brain. By relaxing and opening up to the universe, you may tap into an energetic flow to deliver a seemingly effortless solution. This is part of the magic of getting outside of yourself! We'll further explore nature's role in our well-being later.

ÁINE, THE IRISH GODDESS OF SUMMER

Áine, the Irish goddess of summer, is queen of the faeries! Known by many names, including Áine of Knockainy, Ain of the Light, and Ain Cliar the Bright, she is a sun goddess, moon goddess, and goddess of love. She is celebrated on Midsummer's Eve with festivals and a special feast. Farmers would bring torches of straw to seek protection and fruitfulness for the fields.

Also known as Lady of the Lake, and goddess of Earth and nature, she connects to all the elements. She represents the spark of life and her herb is meadowsweet. As sun goddess, she could walk among her people in the form of "Lair Derg," a red mare who could outrun anything. She lives among the faery kingdom and is a protector of women and animals.

Find Yourself in Your Community

A SENSE OF belonging within a community is something that's gotten a bit lost in today's society, where we all seem to keep our heads down in our own individual flurries of tasks and to-dos. If this resonates with you, why not be a part of bringing community back? You can start small, even with just a vision. Try creating a vision board depicting what this community would look like. How would it feel? Who would be there? What activities would be occurring? Would there be any common goals? Go ahead and visualize yourself participating in an activity with others that feels natural and inspiring for you.

Next, think about aligning your community with your divine gifts. For example, if you enjoy singing or music, find a local choir or musical group. If you're athletically inclined, fitness activities and group sports are a great way to practice self-care *and* community connection. If you are naturally nurturing, put yourself out there as a resource (with healthy boundaries and appropriate compensation, of course). Helping others is one of the most gratifying and fulfilling aspects of the human experience. There are also so many places to volunteer your time. You can serve food at a soup kitchen, visit a home for the elderly, or pitch in at your local animal shelter. As an even smaller but still substantial first step, you can clear out your own space and donate items to a local women's shelter.

When you become involved in a community with like-minded individuals, this can make you feel more empowered to step out as your true self. You may come to feel honored, respected, cherished, and loved by yourself and others. Even if your personality is shy, your soul shines so brightly when connecting or giving to others. This inner light is meant to be shared.

Whether you choose to join a preexisting group or bring together a new group of people, you'll quickly see the effects in yourself and others. By cocreating with your inner divinity, you contribute to your own well-being as well as that of your community. As an interdependent society, we make up something that is greater than the sum of its parts. Humans are inherently interactive beings, and even the most introverted among us craves and benefits from the right kind of healthy interaction.

AMATERASU

Of all the predominant religions, Japanese Shinto is the only one with a female chief divinity. Amaterasu is a sun goddess and her name means "great shining heaven." Shinto recognizes nature spirits and sacred power (kami); thus, she is associated with all of the elements. The unpretentious architectural sites in her honor portray her as the central mirror. As the ruler of all deities, she guards the people of Japan and is the symbol of cultural unity. Her emblem is the rising sun.

Considered to be the ancestor of humanity, her symbol still flies high on the Japanese flag. Legend has it that she once quarreled with her brother, ruler of storms. She did not like his drama and hid away in a cave. The world was then without sun. Desperate for her light, all the other divinities strategized to lure her out of her cave. Don't wait to be lured out of your cave with divine strategies—shine your light now! The world is waiting for you.

Tap into Your Support Systems

WE IDENTIFIED YOUR support system in chapter 1 (see page 15). Your support system is similar to your relationship with yourself, in that it's necessary to nurture it, prioritize it, and be able to trust it. With a qualified, loving support system, you can open yourself up to unconditional love and receive gifts from the universe from a place of strength and confidence. Your support network won't be perfect. We are all human, and people will make mistakes. But when your foundation is strong, and you have various sources of support, you will be able to weather any storm. You always have the option to forgive, or even say goodbye to someone if you need to.

Everyone's support network will look different, but let's explore three areas of life where our relationships are integral for our well-being: friendship, family, and work.

FRIENDSHIP

AS YOU LEARN to feel secure in what you choose to accept for yourself, you can more confidently build solid friendships and nurture them without feeling depleted. In fact, whatever you give of yourself within safe, caring, and trusted connections, you'll usually get in return.

When you think of your friends and those people you usually turn to for giving and receiving support, ask yourself whether these relationships are symbiotic, or mutually rewarding. Quality matters over quantity. If you consistently give more than you receive and it saps your energy, know that it is okay to create some distance with that person. We all have our own paths, and ultimately only we can walk our own. If you have lent enough of yourself to someone else's journey, remember that path is theirs to walk, not yours.

By taking charge of your own health, you can be the one to put an end to repeated negative relationship patterns. This also clears your energetic space to start inviting in healthier interactions. You have this one lifetime in this body and this experience. Your time is valuable, and you deserve to be valued. You get to choose what you are willing to accept for yourself, and it starts by recognizing your own worth.

Some people like to have a few close friends and lots of acquaintances. Some people like to have a central group. It will be different for each person; there is no right or wrong. All that matters is that you feel safe and secure to be true to, and grow, as yourself. True friends are treasures.

Take a moment to acknowledge those who are most special to you. Make a list of your trusted friends in your journal, and write lines of gratitude for each person and their unique gifts. Reflect on what they bring to your life and how their presence and support have shaped your well-being. Remind yourself that these people are always there for you.

If you haven't connected for a while, take some time to reach out. If there has been a rupture in the bond with a dear friend, and you know their heart is usually in the right place, consider taking some extra steps to try and understand what happened and repair the friendship from a place of trust.

FAMILY

IT MAY SEEM like we don't get to choose our family. But some believe that we actually chose them before we got here; that we have soul contracts to fulfill unresolved karma with the family that we are born into in this lifetime. Karma does not need to be seen as good or bad, but rather an opportunity to work through unresolved soul work. In this belief, resisting what comes your way can cause greater friction and frustration, and can lead your soul to repeat the karmic cycle again until you get it right. By gaining the perspective to address a situation head-on, you may be able to break a cycle once and for all.

Another perspective from which to consider family connections is that the family as a collective is working on healing wounds that have been passed on generationally. These wounds may be associated with various unhealthy dynamics, such as dominating, egocentric energy, lack of secure early attachment (meaning disorganized/disoriented, anxious/ambivalent, or anxious/avoidant styles of attachment), addictions, or fear-based mentalities. These wounds may have originated or been perpetuated as survival mechanisms during times of crisis, such as war, famine, or financial depression. Other wounds may come from generational trauma or systemic oppression. It can take generations to work through inherited patterns, wounds, and karma—but each generation offers the opportunity for a new step toward healing.

No matter what you believe regarding your family, you do have choices. You can choose how you engage with them. You can set your own boundaries. You can even choose friends to be your family. If you struggle with your immediate family, you can reach out to extended family to serve as a source of support, to help you remember who you are and your purpose in this lifetime. If you had a warm and loving upbringing that helped you develop a strong, healthy foundation that enables you to generally feel safe as yourself out in the world, then that is terrific. A strong bond allows you to honor your family and your shared life experience.

Maybe some of your family or chosen family members have passed on. Grief is one of the most complex and painful human experiences, and can shake you to your core. Many believe that our spirits are eternal. People you once knew in this life, as well as ancestors you've never met, may be waiting for you to ask for their support. If you feel comfortable, you may even open yourself to the support of your spiritual family in the form of guardian angels or spirit guides (see page 16). This will only ever feel positive or loving.

Spend five minutes writing in your journal about your familial sources of support, whether this includes your immediate family, extended family, chosen family, ancestors, or spirits of others who have passed on. Reflect on how this familial support complements the support of your network of friends.

WORK

THERE IS PERHAPS no place where we so consistently share our gifts and seek the support of others than the workplace. Some work cultures are positive and supportive; others have competitive cultures or foster negativity. If you easily pick up the energy of others, it can be hard to work in close quarters with unsettling or negative energy. In this case, creating a safe space for yourself at work is key to thriving and protecting your energy. You may not be able to achieve your completely ideal environment right away, but you can start by working with what you have and where you are.

First, give yourself permission to set healthy boundaries. This is part of self-care. Addressing your professional boundaries can enhance your productivity and the expression of your divine gifts through whatever you are working on. Spend a few minutes answering these prompts in your journal:

Who are the people in your work environment you trust most to support you?

Who are the people at work who drain your energy?

What boundaries could you set around your interactions with this person or these people?

Are there any changes you could make to your work hours that would improve your well-being? For instance, could you work remotely one day a week? Could you spend time working in a quiet space away from distractions? Brainstorm some ideas in your journal.

Creating a space that inspires you and makes you happy can also be helpful. You can set up physical boundaries with crystals or favorite books as a reminder—to yourself as well as others—that your space is sacred and protected. Think of some ways you could improve your space and list them.

Challenge yourself to implement a new boundary at work this week. If you feel comfortable doing so, talk to your manager about small changes they could support you in making to improve your happiness and productivity at work.

Keep in mind that when you value your workspace and relationships at work, you are honoring your ability to function. And this will reflect in the quality of your work and daily sense of well-being!

Rethink How You Interact with Others

WHEN WE'VE LEARNED to appreciate our own divinity, it can help us recognize the divinity in others. Inner divinity holds kindness and respect for others. It enables us to treat others with compassion and empathy. Let's take some time to think about how you interact with others.

When people are unkind, it is often because of their core wounding. This does not in any way justify their behaviors or their treatment of others. However, considering *why* people behave the way they do can remind us that we are all working on our own issues, and not to take another person's behaviors personally. Unhealthy behaviors or unkind words from another person do not overpower your ability to be true to yourself. You always know your inner truth—no one can take that away from you. You do not have to react. You do not have to engage. Try to have compassion for where the other person is coming from without depleting your own energy on their issues.

It is not generally within our control to change someone else's behavior. It's a waste of energy to try to change someone or live their life for them. Your only real choice lies in your reaction to others. You can't control the behavior of another person, but you can choose to stay away from unhealthy behaviors. Each of us is on our own journey. If you are a parent, teacher, or caregiver for children, you are a role model for them. We should all think of ourselves as role models. What would you like to see in your world? Let your actions set that positive example.

Bullying and gossip serve no good purpose, ever. If you have an issue, the healthiest solution is to address it with someone directly. If you don't know how to handle a situation regarding another person, seek advice from someone you trust or a professional. Thinking about how you would like others to talk about you can help ensure that you only speak about others in the same way. If you feel like someone needs help, find a way to get them the help they need. If you feel like someone is suffering, and it feels right to reach out to them, you can do so in a kind and nonjudgmental way. We are all in this life together. What we put out into the world affects us as well as others. You can be the one to help repair a situation while practicing healthy boundaries and self-care. No step is too small, and no kindness is ever lost.

Experience the Spiritual Benefits of Nature

LET'S GET BACK to nature. There are well-documented health benefits to spending time outside, including decreased stress levels and improved functioning of the autonomic nervous system.

Have you experienced the healing elements of nature?

"Earthing" refers to the simple process of walking outside with your bare feet connected to the earth. It's been found to improve sleep quality and reduce pain. Spiritually, you are grounding your energy, which may help you feel more relaxed, stable, and balanced. Scientifically, you are allowing electrons from the earth to transfer to your body.

The term "forest bathing" (*shinrin-yoku* in Japanese) is the practice of spending quiet time among the trees. It has been associated with mindfulness, mood enhancement, and a strengthened immune system.

The next time you're out in nature, try earthing or forest bathing, and see what it does for you.

When you do go out, start by breathing deeply. You might feel expansive as you connect to nature and your spiritual self. The energy within our planet that nurtures plants to grow is also a life-giving force. When you connect with this force, you experience healing in your body, mind, and soul. When you receive Mother Earth's energy, your heart chakra radiates a healing frequency that helps you and everyone around you. Don't be surprised if an element of nature like an animal, insect, or plant feels this frequency, and reflects some healing right back to you. Maybe a butterfly or a bird will pause near you. Maybe you will find a feather on your path, or feel a tingling sensation in your body. These can be interpreted as winks from the universe to signal divine support of the healthy path you're walking.

Depending on your openness to nature, you may even feel a connection with the elemental kingdom, such as faeries, earth spirits, or nature angels—whatever you envision on your path. Nature can quite literally open your eyes and expand your horizons. As stewards of nature, we can express our gratitude by tending to the environment, treating her gently, and cleaning up after ourselves.

Further connecting us with divinity is the concept that goddesses are most often depicted as forces of nature. Goddess strengths are usually associated with specific elements, such as fire, air, water, and earth. Because of the duality of nature, such forces can be portrayed as both shadow and light.

In Her Own Words:
Elemental Gifts

How can you interpret your divine gifts in terms of the elements?

Do you have a fiery sense of justice, fierce dedication, or the will to persevere? Fire! Burn bright.

Are you intuitive, sensitive, and full of love and compassion? Let your emotions flow through you like water.

Do you have a bubbly personality that effervesces in social situations? You bring the lightness of air to your community and guide winds of change toward positivity.

Do people love to hug you? Earth Mama, you hold grounding comforts and healing abilities within your very hands.

Spend a few moments reflecting on your character in relation to these four elements. What strengths and shadows become clear when you view the double edge of your powerful forces?

SURRENDER TO SPIRIT

WHEN YOU HAVE given it your all in good faith and circumstances seem to be working against you, this is when it's time
to surrender. It is actually times like this when your soul's
purpose and next steps can become abundantly clear. Even
though circumstances may seem out of your control, you will
know what you are fighting for. Because when your inner fire
becomes ignited in this way, the truth can be illuminated. Align
your fire with the highest good by surrendering to spirit, and an
army of angels will be sent your way.

How do you get into this alignment for the highest good?
It's a lot less work than it might seem. In fact, the real work is
to step aside and open yourself up to receive with faith. You
do not need to go searching to find this spark of light and
hope when you need it the most. Just use your free will to
actively surrender to your higher power, and it will come to
you. When you are in alignment with your higher power, you
cannot go wrong. You will know true alignment when it feels
light, safe, healthy, freeing, and trustworthy.

There is no shame in being human, and the human process
is a journey to be honored. We have a spark of divinity within
us, and we can connect with or even channel our higher
power, but in our human form we do not become it. By being
authentic to our human selves, and respecting a higher power,
we open the space for divine intervention. Part of our true
power is knowing our limits, and divine intervention can lead
to the greatest good of all.

By working with this power in a respectful way, the brightest light can shine through us for the highest purpose. Ultimately, our souls are part of this unity consciousness—divine feminine and divine masculine energy together in balance, perhaps working our way back to our full divinity. The human process is to be honored, even though there will be times in your life when you might question why something is happening *to* you. The empowerment comes with the perspective that maybe it is happening *for* you. Everything that comes your way can be an opportunity for soul growth and reflection on your true purpose. When you align with this true purpose, no matter what circumstance you are faced with, you will feel your wings of freedom. With this personal empowerment, and trust in the power that has your back, you will soar to your destiny.

In Her Own Words:
Your Storybook

For this journaling exercise, imagine yourself as a storybook character. Feminine energy has often been portrayed in stories with profound connections to nature and the animal kingdom. You are your own heroine, but it's nice to have friends along the way. Describe your storybook character and include a spirit animal friend. Explore in depth your character's connection to nature and relationship with the elements. Let your imagination run wild. Now write about it in your journal.

Your Relationship with the World

TAKE A FEW minutes to reflect on your work in this chapter. As you reflect, ask yourself:

* Have you begun to notice any changes in your relationship with the outside world?
* When you used the tools in this chapter to actively engage with others, how did it feel?
* What manageable steps did you take toward manifesting a safe space for interacting with others, your community, and the natural world?
* Did anything new, interesting, or good happen?

Take some time to journal about these things. Be honest, and write down any issues or obstacles that got in the way. As you continue to venture outside of your comfort zone, come back to these tools, practices, and reflections often. They are here to support you in sharing your light.

Now, with the sun warmly supporting your inner strength, the moon illuminating the shadows of your subconscious, and your inner light guiding your way into the world, it's time to let go.

CHAPTER SIX

ℒet Go

Did you grow up with a blueprint in your mind of what you "should" become, based on what others have expected of you? Even if someone has wanted certain things for you with the best of intentions, their life path may differ from yours. Others may have learned important lessons on their path and not want you to have to endure the same mistakes. You can graciously accept this wisdom and still be true to yourself.

To begin, think about what expectations you have internalized, via your environment, family, or society. What ideas of "success" have you absorbed or taken on from others?

Success can be defined differently for each life path. Our paths are as unique as we are as individuals, and feelings of accomplishment will be related to what our souls have set out to achieve. Maybe for some it is more career-based, and for others more relationship-focused. Maybe you love caring for children, or maybe your goal is to help animals be treated with more compassion. Maybe you even had different motivations in previous lifetimes— some feel that our soul's intentions for this lifetime are what we hope to balance out from a past life.

In kabbalah, there is a term called "point in the heart." This refers to a more spiritual path, and it is both something born within and something that can be awakened. Part of reconnecting with your inner divinity is letting go of external influences that do not resonate with you and embracing the uniqueness of yourself.

You can do this without fear as long as you maintain your earthly values and responsibilities. This is your life, and it is a gift to all when you live it as your true self.

When you work with the universe, it is essential to establish a healthy amount of trust in the process and to relinquish the right amount of control. To begin safely letting go, prepare yourself to receive something that might not be exactly what you expected, but may be just what you needed.

Give Yourself Permission

AS YOU DEVELOP your relationship with yourself, remember that you can give the universe permission to assist you, and you can give yourself permission to receive what you need.

Imagine a tree, strongly rooted into the earth. While its roots go deep into the ground to receive nutrients, the branches reach up, as if in surrender, to receive the sunlight. The tree integrates earthbound support and receptive openness.

As you ground into your strong personal foundation and connection to Mother Earth, you will come closer to the roots of your truth. As you let go and open yourself to the process, you will receive your light from the universe. Through this integrated process, you will grow and blossom into your full self.

What are your expectations of who you think you "should" be and what your life "should" look like? Take a minute to reflect on what may have influenced these expectations. Did they come from your deepest soul desires, society's rules, or others who have had a profound impact on your life? Spend five minutes writing in your journal about the expectations you feel within. Give yourself permission to question these things and explore their origin in order to honor your true nature.

BAMYA

Sacredly represented by light and a fire that banishes, Bamya is a Zoroastrian goddess. The goddess of twilight, she brings the hope of day. Her unique presence is a protective force in overcoming shadows and achieving victory. When the sun sets in midwinter in Iran, her presence welcomes Sadeh, the celebration of fire.

The book *Spiritual Body and Celestial Earth* describes the goddess: "Bamya (beaming, radiant), who drives the chariot of Mithra (the sun deity) and the third night after death appears to the sacred soul when Mithra climbs the mountain." She is categorized alongside feminine angels such as Ushahina, angel of the hours between midnight and when the stars come out. Characterized by the term "resplendent," Bamya's brilliant majesty is a symbol of shining bright. Honor your twilight hours, knowing that the stars are on their way to guide you. Receive inspiration for your innermost strength, your inner sun, to shine from the brilliance of your soul.

YOU DON'T NEED APPROVAL

YOU DON'T NEED anyone else's approval. As long as you honor yourself spiritually and act with integrity, you are worthy, approved, good, and acceptable. That's it! All you have to do is be true to your core self. A big piece of this is learning to let go of others' expectations and opinions of you.

You may have been in situations where you felt you needed external approval in order to be loved or recognized as an integral part of society. It is natural to feel this way. Our culture sends many messages about what success looks like, especially in terms of financial, material, educational, and professional gains. Plus, the approval of someone important to you can feel like a green light to keep doing what you are doing.

But by giving someone else the power to approve your actions, and thus control you, you give away your personal power. You, and only you, can define your journey and purpose. The next time you're choosing whether or not to act or pursue a goal, ask yourself where this choice is coming from. Are you being guided by you or an outside influence? Finding that answer gets easier with practice.

What other people think is only that: what they think. Your truth is not determined by someone else's judgment of you. Your truth is determined by your soul and your actions. While it can be helpful to check in with others you trust (like your support network), their thoughts don't define you. You get to choose who you are and how you live. Perhaps true fulfillment comes from the good that you do for yourself and others. Only trust the thoughts of those who can clearly see your truth with a pure heart.

YOU ARE ACCOUNTABLE TO YOU

WE ARE ALL accountable to ourselves. Our actions do affect each other, but we are only responsible for the actions we take. We are all on our own personal journeys within an interconnected society. Being accountable to yourself also means standing up for what is right when necessary. Some circumstances are harder than others, but it is what we do within the circumstances that defines us. When you discover what truly matters to you, that will become your guiding light in any situation. Whatever you are faced with, peace and happiness can be found in the satisfaction of addressing what is on your path with integrity.

|MAGINE |F . . .

For the following scenarios, imagine taking the action truest to your heart. First, name at least three emotions you feel when considering taking each action. With conscious awareness of the possible judgments by others, imagine what would happen if you followed through anyway. After you have fully imagined the scenario, describe the best possible outcome in your journal.

1. You choose to wear your hair, clothes, or other physical adornment *exactly* in the way that best fits your personal truth. This can include paying no attention to these things because they do not interest you, spending a great deal of time on this method of self-expression because it is very important to you, or anything in between. In this situation, what feels right, comfortable, and befitting of you?

2. What truth would you speak? Are you holding back a valuable truth that would set you free? Should you speak up in the name of justice? What would you say?

3. Take a safe, well-calculated risk. What would be a bold step for you toward something you might enjoy? Do you want to start a conversation with someone? Audition for dance or theater? Sing at karaoke night? Why haven't you taken this step in the past? How can you take it now?

Little by Little

ALL OF THESE steps are part of a gradual process of stepping out as your true self. As you go along, continue to check in with yourself and assess where you might be getting stuck. If you start to feel overwhelmed or frustrated, ask yourself: What do you need in order to feel safe enough to let go of outside influences?

Let's practice feeling safe. How do you currently feel when you go outside and interact with the world? To begin this exercise, I would like you to imagine what helps you feel safe when you go out as your true self. As you visualize going outside your door, describe how you see yourself from the perspective of someone who adores you. What anticipation do you feel before you set off to your destination? As you step out toward somewhere that inspires you, imagine the place you are going. What are you going to do when you get there? Describe your dream outing experience, who is there, and how you feel when you arrive. Imagine feeling safe as your true self during this experience. What good things happen? Write down the supportive factors that helped you feel secure in yourself during this imagery. Can you implement any of them today? Also include any necessary real-world precautions to keep yourself safe as you explore new territory.

FORGIVE YOURSELF

LET'S CLEAN HOUSE! In this context, your house is the divine temple of your being. To balance the energetic forces within, we can reflect your light to integrate your shadows. To allow for more harmony within your surrounding environment, you can begin to organize your priorities and reframe any perceptions that clutter your truth.

Let's start with ability awareness. You have innate abilities and how you choose to direct them can be determined by the values and goals which are important to you. Name your abilities and reflect this light all around you as we integrate some shadows.

You may perceive some of your qualities as imperfect. Let's take a moment to celebrate that—it might be an indication of how your soul would like to grow in this lifetime. If anyone were perfect, they would have achieved full spiritual enlightenment and would not be here as a human on the earth plane. So, to honor the gift of your human experience, what would you like to learn and how would you like to grow? Do your perceived flaws interfere with your goals and values? If these "flaws" cause yourself or others harm, you can organize this to be your top priority to begin working on immediately. If it is only your perception that you are flawed in some way and this is causing you distress, check in to determine if your perception is accurate or if you are judging yourself based on external pressures. If you are being too hard on yourself, declutter your truth and embrace your strengths. This contributes to your well-being as well as to a more harmonious, heart-centered, and peaceful world.

If you know you need to work on some area, make it your next priority (after ensuring that you are doing no harm to self or others) to build your strength, learn, or grow in that area.

We are all working on ourselves throughout our lives, so just embrace that this is a healthy part of the process. Welcome your shadows into the light and build up the areas where you would like to direct your focus. Allow your spiritual self to guide your decisions and actions. You always have the answers within. This is hard work, and it is great that you are brave enough to do it!

In Her Own Words:
Embrace Your Uniqueness

What year were you born? In the Chinese zodiac, every year has an animal and one of the five elements (wood, fire, earth, metal, and water). Investigate the animal and element associated with your date and year of birth in Chinese astrology. Write your discoveries in your journal.

Animals come in many different shapes and sizes, each with their own gifts. The elements of earth, wood, fire, water, and metal also vary greatly in their strengths.

Jot down some details of these discoveries that resonate with you and your life experience so far. Notice how different this animal and element can be from other animals and elements. Take a moment to appreciate these differences, and note the abilities of these specific characteristics. Think of the abilities of this animal and traits of your element, and imagine how they can help you thrive and embrace your unique life path.

LET GO OF ANYONE HOLDING YOU BACK

YOU ARE ALMOST ready to fly! We are now going to clear the space to open your wings by tapping into your intuition. Grab a pen and your journal, and give yourself permission to be honest with yourself. Now answer this question with an immediate response:

What or who is holding you back?

Go ahead and write. Don't think too hard. Take as long as you need, and then consider this: Are you held back by something within yourself, or do you feel held back by an individual? If you feel that someone else does not have your best interest at heart, it is time to shed some light on the shadows of this connection. I want you to select all the reasons this connection is still in your life, and write any additional reasons not mentioned here:

※ Guilt

※ Obligation

※ Fear

※ Emotional codependency

※ Financial dependency

※ Anxiety about being alone

※ Other _____

Obligations and responsibilities are important to our personal integrity. But sometimes they go too far and take us from our joy. By illuminating the nature of your connections and bringing honest awareness into your consciousness (instead of leaving them as shadows hidden in your subconscious), you can recognize your true responsibilities. Consider: Do you really have a responsibility to this person? Or could you make some space in the relationship in order to tend to your well-being?

If we take too much accountability for someone else, that inhibits their own soul growth. We do not need to live other people's lessons for them. Part of being accountable for yourself is taking care of yourself. So, thinking about your response to the previous question, how are you balancing your responsibilities for self with your responsibility for others?

Are you living your life with a healthy sense of personal accountability, or have you taken on too much of another person's soul work? Have codependent traits found their way into your relationships? There are many books on how to recognize and heal codependency. See the Resources section (page 167) for some valuable references. Pia Mellody, author of *Facing Codependence*, writes about the key features of a codependent relationship. They include difficulty:

- Experiencing appropriate levels of self-esteem
- Setting functional boundaries
- Owning and expressing one's own reality
- Taking care of one's own adult needs and wants
- Experiencing and expressing one's reality moderately (i.e., from a place of balance)

She also speaks of self-esteem based on external validation, and refers to this as "other-esteem."

If you recognize any of these themes in your relationships, it's important to explore the type of nurturing you received during your early attachment. I've included suggested books on attachment theory in the Resources section; you can also do this work with the help of a professional. Whatever your early attachment looked like, you have the power to rebuild a healthy sense of internal validation and self-love in your relationships today. You can take the steps to foster secure and healthy connections.

In some situations, it's appropriate and healthy to create more distance and physical boundaries. In her book *The Awakened Aura*, Kala Ambrose describes human beings as "essentially made of light and energy." She describes how auras can inter-mingle in close proximity, which can be positively stimulating and enhancing, and/or depleting by drawing too much energy away from another's auric field.

You can create and maintain boundaries by verbally holding your ground and setting the example for how you allow others to treat you. Internal boundaries can be strengthened with self-care and not letting others' words get to you.

As you continue to check in with yourself, your integrity and intuition will tell you where you need to take ownership. It is essential to separate the truth of your soul's path from guilt, fear, insecurity, and unhealthy patterns of codependency. You might not have always felt that you had control of a situation, but now you have the freedom to mend within yourself, and release from your life what is no longer healthy. There is a natu-ral sense of grief that comes with releasing toxic relationships, responsibilities that shouldn't have been yours, and goals that came from others. You are free to honor and process this grief to the fullest. Claim your empowerment through your recogni-tion of how you have responded to what has been asked of you and how you will move forward.

Shake off your feathers, hold your ground, live in your truth, and prepare to lift your spirit.

You have begun releasing your shackles in order to open your wings. To truly be able to fly, though, you must first plant your feet firmly on the earth.

Now it's time to gather strength from your roots. With the support of Mother Earth, let's calibrate your direction.

CHAPTER **SEVEN**

Figure Out Your Purpose

In your process right now, which direction are you facing? Independence, career, friendship, romantic love, caring for children, birthing a baby, adopting a child, or the sacred aging process? Tune back into the Three Faces of the Goddess (page 27). Which face, or phase, is guiding you right now? Where is your soul being called? In this chapter, we'll build on the work you've done to connect with your unique purpose and help you think about broad goals for where you will go next and throughout your lifetime!

Making Choices and Goals from Empowerment

ARE YOU FAMILIAR with the concept of a feedback loop? A feedback loop is a system for maintaining homeostasis, or a stable equilibrium. Such systems are found in nature, and have been applied to understanding psychology. When applied psychologically, one operates within a feedback loop by avoiding discomfort, or going toward pleasure, to reach a sense of emotional peace.

Here is an example: Your friend asks if you would like to go to the movies. It's Sunday and you could use the day to refuel with some quiet time, but you don't want to disappoint your friend. You agree to go and therefore successfully avoid fearing that your friend might be disappointed. However, you just added some additional external stimulation to your weekend in the name of avoiding discomfort. Your family invites you to dinner an hour later that Sunday night. Since you still have not had any quiet time, you are hesitant to go, but you don't want to feel guilty. You go to dinner and avoid feeling guilty, but the next day at work you feel exhausted and depleted. Still, it feels rewarding that you did not have to fear anyone feeling upset with you for letting them down.

Let's investigate this loop. Instead of going toward positive internal feedback (how you would have liked to spend your Sunday), you participated in activities to avoid negative feedback (the internal experience of "negative" emotions). To avoid feeling fear or guilt, you sacrificed your self-care and personal boundaries at the expense of your mental and physical energy. You can imagine how this negative cycle might continue as your exhaustion and depletion increase.

Now let's infuse this same loop with homeostasis: Your friend asks you to go to the movies. You like this friend and enjoy spending time together. You tell your friend how much you enjoy their company and offer a less stimulating activity, for possibly a shorter period of time, like going for a walk. This activity includes your self-care, healthy boundaries, and the positivity of connecting with this friend in a way that works for you. After spending a lovely hour walking together through the park, your family calls to invite you to dinner, which on this timeline is still several hours away. This gives you time to decompress and assess how you feel before agreeing to attend. In the previous situation, the guilt may have come from a combination of you wanting to have family time, but also needing your personal time to refuel. You may have felt guilty at the idea of your "choosing yourself" over your family time. In this situation, you have time to yourself to refuel, check in with yourself, and discover that you are recharged enough to go to dinner without feeling like you have crossed a personal boundary. You get to have family time, and it is not at your own expense.

In both of these situations, the relationships are healthy enough for you to be your true self. But by caring for yourself and asserting your needs, you can have even healthier relationships. The great news is, with the right people, you can keep practicing over and over until you feel comfortable with the process—and the love within your connections will only grow stronger. Approaching things from a positive feedback loop will help you discern where you want to go next, both in small steps throughout your day and big strides throughout your life.

What Makes You Feel Fulfilled?

FOR SOME, SPIRITUAL fulfillment comes more from a sense of purpose than desire. Jyotish, the oldest system of astrology, is derived from the word *jyoti*, which means "light," and is the "science of light." Also referred to as Vedic astrology, this understanding of cosmic influences at the time of one's birth can offer suggestions regarding what might be fulfilling to an individual's soul growth and expression.

Your natal birth chart takes into account not only the time you were born but also the physical location. Each planet was in a particular position for your birth. Even the constellations of your planetary placements were in particular alignments with other constellations. The more specific you get with the details, the more your chart may feel tailored just for you. You are a lot more nuanced than just your sun sign (the well-known 12 signs of the zodiac). I recommend researching your natal birth chart and seeing what magic appears. You'll likely recognize many traits and characteristics, as well as yearnings or callings you may not have tuned into yet. If you know the time, date, and location of your birth, you can get your birth chart for free online (I've included some websites in the Resources section on page 167).

Earlier, we discussed the concept of growing up with a blueprint in your mind of what you felt you had to become in order to receive safety, security, love, or abundance. Think of your cosmic alignments as your starprint. While it's important to retain a sense of practicality as you align with your cosmic starprint, you can also welcome a sense of magic. Based on your astrological chart, what might spiritual fulfillment feel like to you?

Nurturing your passions fuels your inner flame. What lights you up inside? What calls out to you louder than your to-do list? Find the pearl of wisdom inside the shell of procrastination—what tasks do you gravitate toward, and which do you put off? What fulfilling things lure you away from your mundane tasks? Take a minute to recognize what these things are and what they have in common. Then, take some time to appreciate that these are things you enjoy and therefore are worthy of your time.

Fulfillment might come from your deeply rooted spiritual purpose. This may be something you have always felt on some level but never fully understood. You may have gone through what has been called a "dark night of the soul," or a spiritual awakening. If you feel called to share your wisdom or healing gifts, this might bring you the satisfaction of following the call of your soul. As you build goals for the future, be guided by your starlight!

What Matters to You?

Take a moment to think about what lights you up. The things that matter deeply to you are where your true purpose lies. In your journal, write answers to the following prompts:

I feel most fulfilled when . . .

A memory that brings me joy is . . .

I always seem to make time for . . .

The tasks that keep me fully engaged are . . .

I feel most myself when . . .

I feel most energized when . . .

ᴅEVI ꙅARASVATI

Devi Sarasvati, "the flowing one," is the personification of the sacred river bearing the same name. The Hindu water goddess of creativity, music, knowledge, and learning, she radiates wisdom. Sarasvati is the Shakti (enlivening female force) the creator Brahma needed for the world to come into being.

She is known to be the inventor of arts and sciences; her eloquence and elegance inspire music. She created words so that songs could be written. Scholars, filmmakers, and musicians call to her for assistance and to honor her. She is part of a trinity, or Tridevi, including Lakshmi and Parvati. Together, they keep the world in balance.

Surrounded by swans, enrobed in light garments (brilliant with enlightenment), Sarasvati resides upon a lotus-blossom throne. Offering others her knowledge, she is believed to have created the Sanskrit alphabet and mathematics. The vina, an Indian lute, is her sacred instrument. Welcome her wisdom to help reveal the true essence of yourself.

What Do You Value?

VALUES ARE THE principles we live by and can be incorporated into our personal goals. While goals differ depending on life circumstance, values tend to remain consistent over a lifetime. For example, at this stage of your life, you may prioritize your goals to have fun, seek new experiences, create a loving partnership, grow your career, focus on caregiving, or increase your financial abundance.

Your goals might change throughout your life. Yet, whatever goals you choose to pursue, your values determine your character. These values act as your internal compass for the manner in which you strive toward your goals.

Here are some questions to help you clarify your values:

When you feel metaphorical murky water all around you, which values help you feel nourished?

- Playfulness
- Spirituality
- Family

- Friends
- Other_____

What inspires your leaves to rise up toward the sun?

- Mental clarity
- Partnership/relationship

- Career focus
- Other_____

What is your lily pad that helps you rest easy?

- Financial abundance
- Health

- Service to others
- Other_____

What helps you find direction in times of unsettled weather?

- Determination
- Faith

- Courage
- Other_____

Think about your answers. Spend a moment writing in your journal about why you answered this way.

Values and Astrology

Western astrology depicts 12 categories of values, represented by the 12 houses. In simplified terms, these include: self, money, the mind, home and family, playfulness, health, legal partnerships, transformation, travel, career, role in society, and spirituality.

Examining the houses in your birth chart may help you figure out which values have been prominent during past challenges, in your lifelong personal traits, and in any life-transforming situations.

You can see how planetary patterns of movement activate certain parts of your chart in real time by visiting astrological websites like Astrolada.com. On her website, Lada Duncheva offers a free birth chart and a personal transit calculator for your upcoming week. Your planetary transits may highlight the values that are coming into focus for you and your current goals.

Though some astrological aspects may highlight support and some others signal a challenge, it is all toward facilitating your soul growth in this lifetime. It's just kind of a heads-up, because you always have free will. Sometimes when we have a sense of what could be headed our way, it can help us be prepared.

CONFLICTING VALUES

JUST BY UNDERSTANDING that we all have different values that become prominent at different life stages, we can focus more clearly on our own journey. What is important to you may not be as important to someone else. Of course, it is of utmost importance to be kind, ethical, and moral in terms of how we treat one another. Beyond that, personal values are up to an individual.

This is where healthy boundaries come into play. It might feel better to surround yourself with people who have similar values to you. You will likely feel a deep and natural connection to those who share your values. But it can also be beneficial to form relationships with those whose values are complementary to yours—this can foster healthy growth around your goals. For example, if you love to care for the earth, and a partner enjoys business interactions, you could be a great match to start an environmentally friendly company. In this situation, both people can have the experience of fulfilling their soul calling, while also honoring complementary values.

At times, our values will conflict with another person's. Say you have a romantic partner who loves going on adventures, while you value quiet time at home. When you agree on the value of your partnership as the top priority, you can take steps to compromise at a healthy level (remember the feedback loop exercise on page 108), and share some activities that are valued by the other in a manner that maintains your integrity, and vice versa. A healthy partnership holds respect for each person's values, as well as one another's necessary boundaries and self-care.

However, some values are never to be compromised. Core values are central to the survival of humanity. It is one thing to value an activity, and quite another to uphold core values such as trust, honesty, and respect. If values that serve the good of humanity and the integral functions of a relationship become a source of conflict, it's time to take careful stock of your values and stay true to them. People must be held accountable for their actions, especially where core values are concerned. When there are disagreements concerning a difference in values, try to have open conversations toward reaching an agreement. While you can continue this conversation, do it with the healthy boundaries you need to uphold your own values and self-care. If you can't find the compromise or respect needed in this situation, consider taking some space from the relationship.

In Her Own Words:
Describe Your Values

What do you value? Describe something you value and how it fulfills you. For example, a favorite song, a long run, satisfaction from solving a math problem, or emotional warmth from a connection with another person. Reflect on the following questions in your journal:

In what ways have you been compromising your personal values to please others?

Describe other values that could be complementary to your values.

Imagine an ideal partnership that holds respect for your values. What does it look like? Feel like?

Explore how your values can be gifts to the world.

Start Thinking about Goals

LET'S BE COMPLETELY honest—no one's watching and no one's listening. What do you *really* want? The world is your oyster, so what is your pearl?

Take a moment to ask yourself: If you could go anywhere, do anything, be any version of yourself, what would that look like? We'll discuss logistics later. But for now, let your inner vision go the distance. There are no limits. Spend five minutes freewriting your answer in your journal.

It's Personal

Because we all have unique life purposes, goals and values will appear differently for everyone.

Think of Artemis and Sedna. In Greek mythology, Artemis was a virginal huntress moon goddess who protected animals, reproduction, and the birth process. Sedna, Inuit goddess of the sea, maintained laws regarding animals in the food chain and determined whether her people would receive a bounty from their hunters or starve. Said to be half-woman, half-fish, she was in charge of the sea creatures.

While both of these beings occupy roles of protection, they play out different divine purposes. The goals and values that concern one do not necessarily serve the other.

You have your gifts and life story. If you believe in such, your goals and values in this lifetime may even be different now than they were for you in other lifetimes. What is important for you to do? Recognize it and claim it with integrity. Perhaps the more sovereignty we impart over our own life experiences, the more we are able to contribute to the whole of society.

DIFFERENT PARTS OF LIFE

OUR LIFE IS built around different spheres, including work, social life, spirituality, education, family, and health. In Vedic astrology, life is expressed within four divisions: dharma, or morality; artha, or material abundance; kama, or desires; and moksha, the final liberation or salvation. Let us walk with Devi Sarasvati, Hindu goddess of knowledge, art, creativity, and wisdom, to help reveal the true essence of yourself.

Which goals feel important for you to achieve in this lifetime? In your journal, draw circles representing the main spheres of your life. At the top of the page, write your broadest life goal. This could be something like "the ability to feel at peace in the moment" or "the ability to return to peace at each moment." This goal is about reaching a level of emotional and mental health that aligns with your values and allows you to ride the tides of emotions and situations that come your way. Life will still happen, you will still experience and go through things, but this goal will become your central core that guides you through all of it.

Now, within each of your spheres, jot down a few goals that come to mind related to your life goal. Don't overthink it.

Imagine yourself at the end of your life looking back to this moment. What will help you reach final liberation, or moksha, in this lifetime? Document those things as your goals.

VISUALIZE WHAT YOU WANT

VISUALIZATION EXERCISES CAN be helpful in figuring out what we want, and what it will look like when we get there. Sometimes we are looking for answers for unhealed wounds, validation that we belong, acknowledgment that we have done a good job, feelings of worthiness as our true selves, or unconditional love. What do you dream of receiving? When you can name your deepest needs, set a goal, and detach from the outcome, you are on your way up to the stars.

If we look to the cosmos, we can see the constellation Taurus. This constellation has been visualized as a wild, free-wandering bull named Cerus. He instilled fear with his strength and was ruled by his emotions. One day, as he was destroying flowers in his path, he encountered Persephone, the goddess of spring. She was able to calm the bull, teaching him patience and how to use his strength wisely. Every spring, as the myth goes, Persephone rides on his back across the land, nurturing all the flowers to bloom in their path. She then returns to Hades in the fall, when Cerus returns to the sky as the constellation of Taurus.

What would *your* star story be?

We are going to do a visualization exercise to connect with your inner divinity. If you could see yourself as a constellation, how would your story represent your place in the cosmos? Let's imagine how your immortality might shine throughout the universe. Get ready to light up the night!

1. Create a main character for your constellation and describe this character's personality attributes.
2. What goal does this character seek in the storyline you are envisioning?
3. Describe the setting where the story takes place and any other characters that may be involved.
4. Let the story start to play out, beginning with the character's current situation. What steps does the character take to move toward their goal?
5. Observe the character's behaviors. Try to name the motivations behind why they chose their particular goal and the subconscious needs that might drive their actions.

6. Put an obstacle in the way!
7. What are the thoughts, emotions, or inspirational hopes that encourage the character to persevere toward their goal, despite the obstacle?
8. Do any friends show up along the way to help out?
9. For this next part, take a deep breath, release control, and hold a space with faith to allow for an image to come to you. Allow this next visualization to come to you in whatever form it takes.
10. With the first image that comes to your mind as a guide, imagine a positive outcome.
11. Does the character attain what they set out to achieve or something different?
12. Describe the immortal values of this story and imagine how it is depicted in a constellation of stars that lives on for eternity.

In part 3, we'll look at self-care, self-love, and your personal goals. As the flame of your personal sun empowers your sense of purpose, and the soft glow of moonlight invites your feminine divinity out of the shadows, secure your true north and get ready to take your place among the stars.

PART **THREE**

How You'll Get There

As you continue doing the work to embrace your unique starprint, we will fuel your journey with divine self-care and self-love. This can help you remember who you are, and who you came here to be. It is time to care for your wings of divinity and let your spirit soar.

Your fears no longer have the power to hold you back. You have clarity about who you are and what you want. You are releasing what no longer serves you, so you can walk your path toward your goals with freedom and in truth. You are reclaiming your spiritual self!

CHAPTER **EIGHT**

ENGAGE IN DIVINE SELF-CARE

Self-care enables us to function as our true self, form sustainable relationships, show up as our full self, and maintain healthy boundaries. Divine self-care helps us shine even brighter. In this chapter, we'll explore the different facets of self-care and how to create a routine that works for you. This is a huge part of your journey going forward, one that will reap endless rewards!

What Is Divine Self-Care?

SELF-CARE IS ANYTHING that allows you to prioritize your mental, emotional, spiritual, and physical health. It's about considering your own needs and being your best self so you are able to show up for others in a healthy and fulfilling way. It can include activities such as exercise, meditation, and hobbies. Most importantly, it is something that is healthy and restorative to *you*.

Take a minute to feel proud of who you were born to be, and all the work you have done to get to this point. Self-care is an ongoing process. It will feel different depending on your life stage and current circumstances. Continually check in with yourself about what you need in order to refuel and live as your best self. As your needs change, you'll want to adapt your self-care practice. Self-care requires being in tune with yourself and giving yourself just the kind of love you need at any moment in time. It's beautiful because it comes from *you*. It is not dependent on others. No matter what is going on in your life, you can always take a moment to take care of yourself.

In Her Own Words:
What Kind of Flower Would You Be?

What kind of flower best describes your nature? Once you've selected your flower, grab your journal and draw it, paste a photo of it, or press a physical specimen of the flower.

Consider the beauty of the flower. Examine all the individual and unique qualities you can find. List them. Now view yourself from this lens. List out all the ways you are beautiful, special, and unique. As a flower, you know the nutrients you need to bloom. Make a list of all the "nutrients" of self-care you need in order to grow, thrive, and reach toward the light.

SELF-CARE SETS YOU UP FOR SUCCESS

WHEN YOU VALUE and care for yourself, you create your own inner wellspring of primal life force energy. This keeps you energized and motivated toward achieving your goals and accepting only healthy relationships for yourself.

Self-care can lead to inner peace and contentment. When your well is full, you will not need to seek the springs of external validation of others. This gives you more time and energy for building on your personal integrity and core values, and doing what you are meant to do in this life.

Our behaviors influence the behaviors of those around us. When you value and care for yourself, you will model this for others. You will be a reminder that we are all divine beings and worthy of our time here on Earth.

Working toward your goals and living with purpose is an act of self-care in itself. Keep the space open to receive by caring for yourself and maintaining your well.

BURNING OUT

WE'VE ALL EXPERIENCED burnout at some point or another. It comes in many forms, such as physical or emotional exhaustion, loss of inspiration or hope, decreased empathy and compassion, and even diminished ability to function. At first glance, you might not see it for what it is—on the surface, burnout can look like procrastination, excuses not to go to work, being less than kind to others, or lack of patience. It can often affect the quality of whatever you are working on.

On a deeper level, burnout can be a signal that your well is empty, and that you are disconnected from your divinity. When we are not actively, consciously aware of where our energy goes, it can be taken from us far too easily.

Healers often encounter burnout because they are so used to caring for others. It may feel unnatural or selfish to take time out for self-care. That is why it's so important to realize not only the necessity but also the value of making sure you have what you need to stay in balance. Particularly for spiritual and emotional healers, it is very important not to absorb what you are working with others to heal. That energy needs to be actively transmuted and released out of your system. I've included some guides in the Resources section (page 167) to help you manage this.

By proactively practicing healthy self-care, you can check in with yourself, give yourself what you need, and prevent burnout. Taking those steps now will prevent you from having to face the consequences later of not functioning at your best. If you do find yourself in a state of burnout, take time to pause. Check in with yourself. Identify the ways you need to care for yourself, even if that means seeking professional help. With time, self-care, and compassion, you can fill your well back up.

It's Spiritual, Physical, Mental, and Emotional

DIVINE CARE INCLUDES care for the entire self. Therefore, any approach should address the needs of the mind, body, spirit, and soul. What does this look like?

Spiritual self-care refreshes your spirit in whatever way is right for you. This could be a religious practice, but it doesn't have to be. It could also include meditation, yoga, breathwork, reading spiritual texts, or visiting a spiritual place.

Physical self-care is taking care of your body by finding a physical activity that works for you, like walking, running, hiking, going to the gym, or doing yoga or Pilates. When it comes to physical exercise, there are countless ways to help boost your endorphin levels. The healthier we feel, the more our confidence soars. The benefits of movement also include increasing the flow of *qi*, or life force energy. Healthy food is another good foundation for physical health. Ayurvedic medicine is an ancient Indian system that offers ways to nurture your particular physical makeup and body type. There are also diets tailored to blood type, and others that cater specifically to female biology. In the Resources section (page 167), I have included various resources for health and well-being, including an online market that offers fresh and healthy recipes for all kinds of nourishment.

Mental self-care makes sure your mind stays stimulated and continues to grow. This includes anything that helps you learn, such as reading, listening to podcasts, trying a new skill, or games or puzzles that involve problem-solving.

Emotional self-care is anything that helps you get in touch with and reflect on your emotions. You're checking in with yourself. This could involve meditating, getting creative with hobbies, or listening to music in the dark. Journaling or talking to a trusted friend are other simple ways to tend to your emotional health.

As you continue to define your self-care practice, make sure you are addressing all these areas of your well-being.

OSHUN

Oshun, Yoruba goddess of the river, is honored in Nigeria with dancing. She is a goddess of love and is associated with the element of water. Women dance for her, hoping to be chosen as a community advisor for family concerns and to become a healer. Oshun is an Orisha deity of sweet or fresh waters, who delivers water to those in need. She bestows fertility and prosperity as she nurtures humanity. Her emblem is the brass bracelet.

When her spirit moves through dancers, it is as though they are swimming through sacred waters. A teacher of mysticism and agriculture, she is known for the art of divination. Think of her loving nature when you want to feel safe, as you do what you need to do for self-care. She offers protection through her being and is a bringer of song. Sometimes she has been depicted as a mermaid! Sing and dance with her.

IN HER OWN WORDS:
Lightning in a Bottle

Imagine yourself as a firefly. On a warm summer evening, you get trapped in a bottle. You don't know when or how you will get out. Find the inner spark where your light shines and listen to it. What does it say to give you hope? Take that spark of hope and turn it into a bolt of lightning. Break out of the bottle and fly. Carry that spark of hope everywhere you go and light up the night.

FIGURING OUT WHAT WORKS FOR YOU

IN YOUR JOURNAL, map out the specific ways you will tend to the four realms of your self-care practice. Include the activities and approaches that feel best for you today.

Now ask yourself, how can you start and stick to these practices? We know what is good for us, but sometimes we end up relying on old habits or reaching for the quick fix. This is where routine comes into play. With a self-care routine, you train your brain as well as your physical body, so your healthy choices soon become your habits. For example, try building into your morning routine a 20-minute yoga video or nature walk. After a couple weeks, you won't even think about starting your day without this self-care practice!

The smaller the steps, the less overwhelming it will be to create a routine and stick to it. Start small and get specific, and trust that what you are doing is good for you.

For example, set out to research the ideal daily diet for your body, mind, and soul. Once you identify the ingredients you need, the next step could be to set up a menu for the week. Once your week begins and you reach for that quick fix, you'll already have a delicious and healthy alternative ready to go.

It takes dedication to stick to a routine, which is why creating a plan is worth it. To create a plan that works for you, think about what you're feeling and what you need most right now. Would you like to increase your confidence? Feel more fulfilled on an internal level? Add some sweetness to your life? Tap into more inspiration and motivation? Acknowledge what you are craving to help you decide what your routine should look like.

Map out a loose self-care routine in your journal. Feel free to add to it and change it over time—it's always a work in progress.

Your Own Self-Care Intervention

Check yourself into pre-hab! Don't wait until all of your resources are depleted to reach for help from within. Intervene for yourself and take control of your self-care situation. What do you need to pre-recover from burnout? Time alone in nature? Lunch with a friend? A babysitter? Though it may be hard to justify the cost of prevention, think of it as way less expensive than undoing whatever happens down the line when you are not your best self.

Grab your journal and fill in the blank: I feel most refreshed when . . .

Get back into the flow. Do you feel like whatever you are trying to do comes up against a brick wall? Are you forcing something before its natural timing? Do things in your world just feel extra difficult? Hard work and dedication are excellent and necessary qualities, but make sure you're working with a full tank! Take a break, take a breath, and surrender. Do something you enjoy, and don't be surprised if in some subtle way it gets you back on track.

Fill in the blank: I enjoy myself most when . . .

Make a wish. What do you wish you could do, if you were living from your spiritual self and had all the abundance in the world? Now envision a dandelion and see a wish, not a weed. As you blow those magical seeds into the wind, imagine your wish coming true. What's one thing you can do right now to plant a seed for that wish?

Fill in the blank: I wish I may, I wish I might . . .

IDENTIFY YOUR STRESSORS

WHAT ARE YOUR biggest stressors? Thinking about these can also help you figure out what types of self-care are best for you to focus on.

Examining your coping mechanisms and cravings can help you figure out what your stressors are. For example, when do you find yourself reaching for chocolate? Chocolate has been shown as beneficial to balancing female hormones. So, if you're reaching for chocolate, how is your adrenal system? If you're upping your coffee intake, are you getting adequate rest? If you're having trouble sleeping, are you getting enough exercise during the day?

Identifying our stressors and their associated habits can serve as great clues into where we might need more self-care.

SET BOUNDARIES

WE'VE TALKED AT length about healthy boundaries; they are a powerful form of self-care. For example, say someone you haven't seen in years is coming to your town for a visit. They ask if they can stay with you for a week. You let them know that this isn't a good time, or invite them to come over for dinner and spend one night. Nice work—you've set boundaries!

If your boundaries were violated in the past, you may have made yourself believe that you can't set boundaries or that boundaries are flexible. It may be difficult to realize that you're allowed to say no to things. Start by giving yourself permission.

Boundaries help you retain your own energy and stay healthy. Have you ever known someone who just seemed to take up all your energy? These people are called "energy vampires." They're people who take up a lot of emotional bandwidth. They always want to talk to you about their feelings, and they are often embroiled in drama. A key characteristic of emotional vampires is that they often don't reciprocate. They may not even consciously know that they are doing it, and you may not even consciously be aware that it is happening. If you have ever felt drained or depleted around someone, there's a good chance they were using you as a source of energy without even realizing it. Maybe you help lift their spirits or support them emotionally. This is fine when you practice healthy self-care and know when to set limits. However, if you become resentful after giving too much, it's healthier to set boundaries and protect your energy.

Another great way to cultivate boundaries is to spend some time alone. Everyone should be able to feel good in their own company. It's a good practice to work on this regularly. You can do this by checking in with yourself in your home environment at any time. Just bring to conscious awareness how you feel when you are alone. When you work on finding your inner source of happiness, your sense of self will benefit, and that joy will magnify when you are around others.

It may be tough to start setting boundaries, but they are beneficial and empowering in the long run. Healthy boundaries free up your time and space, empowering you to make choices in how you want to live *your* life. Friendship is meant to be a safe place to share thoughts, emotions, and experiences. When you trust someone, you can share burdens in confidence, and have each other's best interest at heart. You can give freely, knowing that it comes back in an even brighter form.

SAY NO WHEN YOU NEED TO

IN ORDER TO maintain healthy boundaries, you may need to practice saying no. First, understand that you are allowed to say no. You have total permission to decline what does not feel right to you.

Think of an invitation or situation to which you would like to say no. What might your intuition be trying to tell you? Go ahead and process this by writing in your journal. While you're writing, keep in mind that your worth, your value, and your time are precious. You are the only one who can set these boundaries, so it's up to you.

When something feels right to you, it will not feel draining to say yes. Sometimes it takes time to get to this place, because first you have to practice self-care to refill your well. The further along you get with your self-care, the more you will be able to fulfill your responsibilities with a sense of joy and integrity. You will know how to say no, and also have more energy for the activities to which you have said yes. A "no" to someone or something else is often a "yes" to you.

BE CLEAR ABOUT YOUR NEEDS

AS YOU CONTINUE setting boundaries and listening to what you do and do not feel comfortable with, you'll want to focus on communicating your needs to others. As your internal compass leads the way, you can assert your needs with confidence that you are headed in the right direction. You can speak up for yourself and prioritize your spiritual, emotional, and physical needs. Trust that others will assert their own healthy boundaries and stay focused on finding the right resources for yourself.

What Self-Care Isn't

Self-care is not external validation. *It isn't putting makeup on so that other people will recognize our value; rather, it's the time we take being comfortable with ourselves and feeling good in our own skin.*

Self-care is not mindlessness. *It is important to relax, but mindfulness holds the space for the dignity that we all deserve. Relaxing is not a free pass to be irresponsible, gossip, or be unkind in any way; few activities can snuff out our inner light as effectively as these.*

Self-care is not superficial. *When we do something for our body, the best reward is how it makes us feel on the inside, not superficial gains.*

Self-care is not taking others down to build ourselves up. *We can defend ourselves and stand strong as we are, but there is no point in actively taking down another. We find our greatest strength in how we stand alone, not how we compare to others.*

Self-care does not discriminate. *Everyone is worthy of self-care. Keeping humanity in mind is part of self-care, because we are all one. We can make the world better by taking only what we need and giving what we can give.*

Build on the Basics

OF ALL THE things that ground us, the essential basics of getting enough sleep, deep breathing, eating healthy, drinking water, and having an active routine will always support any self-care journey.

Earlier we discussed how breathing connects our spirit to our body. There are many types of breathing exercises that not only calm and center, but also have spiritual benefits. For example, *nadi shodhana pranayama* is a breathing exercise that helps clear the mind and body. (The Sanskrit name roughly translates to "channel" or "flow" and "purification.") This is done by alternating nostrils when inhaling and exhaling. The practice aims to balance masculine and feminine energies.

Sleep is essential for physical and mental health, and it also helps connect us to our divine purpose. Information received from the dream state can help guide us in the physical realm. Like meditation, dreaming can connect us to our intuition and sense of inner peace. During the dream state, we can receive symbols that indicate what the ego is trying to block, or what might be hard to look at in our waking state. Processing these symbols can help shed light on the messages and shadows within the subconscious self.

Prioritizing these aspects of your health, in addition to creating a nutrition and physical movement routine, will do wonders for your well-being. Once you discover what all these things can do for your holistic health, you'll be even more motivated to stick to your self-care practice. As you begin to repeat healthy patterns, healthy neural pathways will form and solidify. As a result, self-care will become much easier.

Through self-care you will learn to love yourself even deeper. In the next chapter, we will look to the stars for your path to divine self-love.

CHAPTER **NINE**

Practice Fearless Self-Love

Now that we've explored how to provide proper self-care, it is time to love yourself without fear! This chapter dives into principles and practices that allow self-love to flourish. When you live from a place of self-love, you will have the time, space, and energy to do what you love and spend time with the people you love. Self-love radiates out to every area of your life! Let's take a look.

Love Yourself

YOU HAVE ALWAYS been capable of self-love. The more you create a safe space to connect with what and whom you love, the more love you will feel. The more you value yourself, the more confident you will feel in allowing others to appreciate your value. The more you live from your truth, the less open you will be to anything coming from anyone else that does not belong to you. Be the gift that you are. Don't let anyone who deserves you miss out because others have tried to take from you. Stand tall and proud.

Everything that we have worked on so far—getting in touch with yourself, focusing on your strengths, and cultivating self-care—has brought us to self-love. Distractions will come, but this is where all your work will keep you strong. The muscles you have been building your whole life are now redirected toward *your* goals. The routine you have been repeating is creating healthy new patterns for you. You can now trust where you are going and that you will get yourself there. It will become more and more natural to continue on your path. You know how to get back up again when you have to—and you know you will have to—and you are prepared.

THAT MEANS ALL OF YOURSELF

SELF-LOVE APPLIES TO our whole self, flaws and all. No one is perfect. When we judge ourselves too harshly, we are creating feelings opposite to love. When you love yourself, you can come to accept yourself as you are and continue to work toward your goals. This is the power of shadow work (see pages 43 and 62). Once you can embrace your whole self, it's easier to let go of what doesn't matter and have a lot more fun in life.

What Is Divine Self-Love?

DIVINE SELF-LOVE MEANS honoring your inner divinity, and the life you came here to live. It is a fearless love based on all you've done to connect with your true light and to care for yourself. Self-love allows you to speak your truth, use your voice, or just say no.

A big part of divine self-love is prioritizing yourself and your own needs. The more you get to know yourself, the more you will be able to recognize when you do not deserve certain treatment from others. You get to choose who you let into your life, and you choose how you will be treated. For example, how do you feel when you go to certain events? Do certain social situations make you uncomfortable? Since you cannot control anyone's behavior but your own, feel empowered by how much control you have over yourself. Stay focused on feeling good by removing yourself from situations that do not feel right, or stepping away from conversations that are not kind. Just politely excuse yourself. You may also gently speak your truth before politely excusing yourself, but that's up to you. Some conversations are difficult to have but are necessary for creating a just society. The more you feel comfortable engaging in these conversations, the more we as a society can grow together.

As you begin to shine and feel more comfortable with yourself, others will notice. Some will like this, and some will not. Expect a variety of responses. But as long as you keep growing in self-love and surround yourself with people you trust, others' opinions will matter to you less and less. Self-love builds on itself!

SELF-LOVE IN ACTION

Have you ever trusted a product just because it came from your favorite brand? Have you ever been excited to listen to a new song just because you already love the artist? Have you ever valued advice just because you admire the person who said it? The reason you trust and love these things is because you appreciate where they come from.

You are a creator, too. There will be people who trust, love, and value what comes from you just because you're you. As you create your life, know that you have something very special to offer the world. Be the first to honor this within yourself. Self-love is like your own personal generator. It fuels everything you do.

Reflect on the following prompts in your journal:

What are the special qualities that make you, you?

What do the people in your life tend to love and admire most about you?

What do you have to offer the world that comes directly from your spiritual self?

Come back to these answers whenever you need a boost of self-love. Here are some mantras you can repeat anytime you need a loving reminder:

Divinity is my birthright.
My path is beautiful.
My voice matters, and I have important things to say.

Prioritize Your Own Happiness

WE ARE ALL allowed to be happy.

Happiness and contentment are signals that you are on the right path. When you're happy, it's an expression of joy that is one of the highest vibrational frequencies.

Prioritizing happiness is also a way of staying in tune with your intuition. It can help you figure out what is or isn't working with your self-care. Of course, there will always be challenging circumstances that are out of our control, and we will always face boring or tedious responsibilities that may not make us happy on an immediate level (like taking the car in for an inspection or walking the dog in a torrential downpour). We can't be happy all the time. The human experience embraces both joy and struggle. But if you find yourself in a stretch of unhappiness or feeling distant from divine self-love, check in with your self-care routine. Often when we are in a rut, it's because we've fallen out of the routine of caring for ourselves.

Checking in with our relationships is another way to prioritize our happiness. In certain relationship dynamics, you may feel like you cannot be happy unless you are making someone else happy. But as we've discussed, it is not our job to make other people happy. It *is* our job to hold our values and treat others with kindness. It is up to each individual to find their own happiness. What if you are helping others and not feeling happy? This is a big signal that these people may not have your best interests in mind.

As you become secure in your sense of self, you'll create relationships that enhance your happiness. It's okay to release those with whom your relationship is not symbiotic—when it's done with compassion, this is actually an act of radical self-love. Listen to your heart and figure out what's right for you.

THINK ABOUT YOUR NEEDS

WHEN WE DON'T listen to what we need, the messages tend to get louder until we cannot avoid them. Ignoring personal and psychological needs can sometimes even manifest as physical ailments and psychosomatic symptoms. For example, say you really need a break. You haven't used any of your vacation days or sick leave in over a year because you are so dedicated to your job. You feel the urge to take that trip you've always wanted to take, but you keep telling yourself it's not the right time. You keep going to work, and subtle cues of burnout start to arise. You start to feel resentful that you aren't appreciated enough for the sacrifices you make at work, including putting off that trip. And then you get sick with the flu. You are stuck at home in bed, wishing you had taken the trip at your first instinct.

It takes practice to listen to our needs and to address them before they manifest as impulses or harmful symptoms. The best way to do this is to take our own needs seriously in the first place. Women have historically put their needs to the side to care for others. When you live in self-love, you pay attention to your instincts and address your needs when they arise. You do this because you know you are worth it. You're in tune with yourself enough to know you should go ahead and take that trip so you can be restored, rejuvenated, happy, not resentful, and be spared of the flu!

A DAY IN THE LIFE OF SELF-CARE

PRACTICE PAYING ATTENTION to your needs from the moment you wake up. Listen to your body to signal which foods it needs and how to stay hydrated in the proper way. (Ayurveda can help with this; see the Resources section on page 167 for more information.)

As you get ready for your day, review your obligations and see if you can do them with joy, knowing they contribute in some way to your life path. If you can't get past a negative feeling regarding a certain part of your day, check in with yourself. Reflect on what you may need to address around this task. Is it bringing up burnout, complexity in a relationship, or stress? Find one thing you can do to take control of the situation, even if it's just allowing more time for the task or giving yourself permission to put it off for a few days or delegate to someone else.

When you go to bed at night, see if you feel at peace. This is a good time to take out your journal. Write down what has been working for you and what has felt challenging. Reflect on how you can address any needs that are coming up. By doing this, you are honoring the messages from your soul and spirit.

In Her Own Words:
Dreamwork

Are you struggling to find a solution to a lingering problem? Do you have a question you wish you could ask your higher power?

At night, just before you go to bed, write down your problem, question, or difficult emotion. As you fall asleep, willingly surrender it to the universe and request to remember the answer upon waking. Be open to the form this answer may take in your dreams or feelings—it may be symbolic or abstract. In the morning, reflect on any dreams you had and examine them for symbols or subtle answers. Check in with how you're feeling first thing in the morning—sometimes the answer lies just in this feeling.

As you continue to journal about and reflect on your dreams, you'll discover more and more about your subconscious self and the answers you hold within.

GIVE YOURSELF SPACE

WHEN YOUR PHYSICAL, emotional, or spiritual fuel starts to run low, consider it a warning signal. The more depleted we feel, the more susceptible we are to others asserting their needs above ours or taking what they need from us. If we lack the energy it takes to mindfully choose our own actions, it may lead to impulsive reactions.

If you can relate, this is a sign that you need to take some time to yourself. Just like setting boundaries in relationships with others, it is important to set boundaries around having time alone to refuel and reflect. Giving yourself space when you need it is proactive; it gives you the resources to regain self-control. Through space, you center yourself so you can make wise, responsible decisions. Prioritizing time alone to reset will give you the energy and clarity of mind to assert yourself from a place of self-love and mindfulness.

The next time you start to sense that you're running on fumes, stop what you're doing and take a break.

MAKE TIME FOR THE THINGS YOU LOVE

ONCE YOU HAVE created the space to keep your inner furnace burning bright, you get to use your time for the things *you* love!

Don't hesitate to do what you love. A beneficial outcome of self-care is having the time and energy to do what you love, rather than being dragged down by relationships, experiences, and habits that take you away from your true self. When you live from a place of self-love, there are so many possibilities out there for you. All you have to do is walk your path. Start with small things and work your way up. When you do what you love, you send out an irresistible light, and positivity will come right back to you.

VESTA

Vesta lived within the heart of a flame.

Virgil, the great Roman poet, described her as more easily felt than explained. Mysterious and often portrayed with a veil, she is recognized as more of a spirit than any kind of physical embodiment. Vestal virgins, who were priestesses, guarded her eternal flame.

She was a central figure in the original Roman pantheon of deities, and she brought prosperity to the home. With her warmth, she helped renew familial bonds and was often known simply as "mother." Daughter of Saturn, the great teacher planet and ruler of the cosmos, her siblings included Jupiter, Neptune, Pluto, Juno, and Ceres. Ultimately her likeness was renamed in Greek mythology as Hestia. Whatever name you are called, remember that your eternal flame illuminates your true self. With the fire of Vesta, you have the power to transmute, regenerate, and reclaim your divinity.

MAKE TIME FOR THE PEOPLE YOU LOVE

OUR TIME ON Earth is precious; share yours with those you love as much as you possibly can. Spending time with people we love is an extension of self-love. Think how good you feel when you are around your people. This is one of the best methods of self-care, because you are allowing yourself to give and receive love. You have opened up the opportunity to let the sunshine in!

Nurturing your healthy relationships is a way to nurture yourself. If you can balance your time spent with others with the time you make for yourself based on your own needs, your inner well will always be full to the brim.

CRYSTALS AND AROMATHERAPY FOR SELF-LOVE

When you live in your truth and strive to always be kind to yourself and others, you'll want to protect what you're creating. Different forms of healing, such as crystals, stones, and essential oils, can enhance and protect your connection with your spiritual self.

Crystals and stones come from the same mineral kingdom as the ground we walk on, and are believed to have healing and metaphysical properties. The best way to find the ones that work for you is to hold them in your hands and see which ones feel right intuitively. Crystals and gemstones can pick up and hold energy, and this is one way they help you. When you first get yours, you will want to clear their energy by placing them in the sun or by burning sage around them. Keep them "high vibin'" by regularly clearing them and charging them with the sun or moon. You can read more about the different chemical and possible metaphysical properties of crystals and gemstones in many different books (see Resources, page 167). Some of my personal favorites are listed here:

Amethyst: *healing and alchemy*

Apophyllite: *space clearing, energy filtering, third-eye awakening*

Bloodstone: *courage, mysticism, detoxification*

Celestite: *calmness, intuition, serendipity, angelic inspiration*

Chrysocolla: *empowered femininity, grace, intuition, truth*

Lapis lazuli: *rebirth and regeneration*

Obsidian: *grounding and protection*

Quartz: *ambient light*

Sulphur: *happiness, creativity, boosted immunity*

Aromatherapy is rooted in botanical medicine. Plants have been applied throughout history for healing physical, psychological, and metaphysical imbalance. I've included a few of my favorite essential oils, although there are many others, and each has its own powers. You can place a few drops of oil in a diffuser to create a healing atmosphere. Use your body wisdom to see which appeal to you:

Bergamot: *uplifting, inspiring, antibiotic, promotes blissful sleep, self-acceptance*

Cinnamon: *analgesic (pain relieving), stimulating, promotes abundance*

Clary sage: *antiseptic, calming, eases menstruation*

Geranium: *love and trust, balancing and harmonizing, regenerative*

Jasmine: *confidence, uplifting, promotes safety, healing, respect*

Lavender: *therapeutic, peaceful, soothing for mind and body*

Myrrh: *grounding, strengthening, rejuvenating*

Rose: *relaxing, soothing, confidence building, love*

BE FAIR TO YOURSELF

A BIG PART of self-love is being fair to yourself as you face your goals, set boundaries, and try new things. Sometimes after you think you've addressed a need around a thought, emotion, person, situation, or feeling, it somehow pops up again. This is normal. By the time something comes up again, take heart in knowing that now you have the skills to address it and release it for good.

The most important thing for you to do is have compassion for yourself when something comes up again. You are not weak; you are human! This is exactly what we are *supposed* to experience: the process. Your strength is found in the work you do and in continuing on your divine path. This is hard for anyone. When you do it with the frequency of love in your system, it keeps your energetic vibration high and attuned to the divinity in others and the world around you. Whenever you misstep, remember that is *part* of the process. It is just as important to know what isn't your path. And, sometimes the very best things happen when you take a detour.

Now let's continue to map your divine path by setting goals and taking steps to achieve them.

CHAPTER **TEN**

Your Divine Path

It's time to walk your path! What will this stage mean for you? Where are you ultimately headed? Let's take some time to document your goals and identify the values that will support you in achieving them. In this chapter, you'll begin taking the steps toward living as your most divinely-guided self. Approach this path with confidence, and remember that you have all the tools you need to continue traveling in the right direction. On you go!

You Are Full of Potential

DO YOU KNOW your own potential? How will you ever find out if you stay on the riverbank? So far, you have been dipping your toes in the water. You are now ready to swim out to the horizon. Invite Anuket to help nourish your journey.

ANUKET

Anuket is the ancient Egyptian goddess of the Nile River. Her name means "embracer," as her arms reach out as two tributaries of the river. She has been revered throughout time for her life-sustaining water and floods that enrich the fields. In gratitude, people have offered her coins, gold, and jewelry. Anuket nourishes abundance and divine strength as you strive to achieve triumph and success.

On the sacred island of Seheil and in the city of Aswan, she was the first goddess of the Nile to rise. She is represented by fast-moving arrows, and her sacred animal is the gazelle. She is depicted wearing a feather headdress in hieroglyphs.

If you see a feather on your path, perhaps it will inspire you to keep forging ahead. Invite Anuket to help you manifest your potential and support your swift momentum in a healthy direction.

It's time to set your sights on your biggest dreams, far out on the horizon, where the earth appears to meet the sky. Channel Anuket, and embrace your journey.

Now is not a time to fear failure. The currents are on your side. You can set your sights to the sun. You are ready to set big goals!

Reasonable Goals

ARE YOU READY for practical magic? Let's set some big, but realistic, goals.

What constitutes a reasonable goal? I like to guide my clients in creating SMART goals. This acronym stands for Specific, Measurable, Achievable, Realistic, and Time-Based. Let's take a look:

Specific means getting as clear as possible about what the goal is. For example, let's say you want to become a social worker. You might start with the specific goal of getting into a master of social work (MSW) program.

Measurable means you have a clear way of knowing when you've achieved this goal. In this case, it would be when you are admitted to an MSW program and begin coursework.

Achievable and Realistic mean that the goal is within your reach. If you don't yet have a college degree, the goal of getting into an MSW program is not yet achievable or realistic for you, and you have a few steps you have to take first. But if you have your bachelor's degree, this is a perfectly achievable and realistic goal.

Time-based means you have a loose time limit on when you will achieve the goal. If you need to choose an MSW program and apply, your time limit would be around one year.

As you work through SMART goals, you take real steps toward reaching your larger goals. The next step in this example would be completing the MSW program, which would take about two years. The next goal could be around getting your license. And eventually you will achieve your ultimate goal of becoming a licensed social worker.

Remember, true goals are about you, not others. A goal wouldn't be to get your mom to quit smoking or your friend to get a better job. While you can have well-intentioned hopes for others, these are not goals.

SHORT-TERM AND LONG-TERM GOALS

AS YOU CAN see with the SMART goals process, it's a good idea to break your bigger goals into smaller steps. Achieving short-term goals along the way builds confidence and motivates you to continue working toward your larger goal. You can also have a mix of smaller individual short-term goals and broader long-term goals.

Short-term goals could be things like: I want to start running in the morning three times a week, I want to start seeing a therapist once a week, or I want to take a class on making French macarons. Even short-term goals can be broken down into smaller steps. For example: I will walk-run a mile for week 1, I will run a full mile for week 2, I will run two miles for week 3, and so on.

Long-term goals tend to focus on big life milestones and take more than a year. These are things like becoming a social worker, going back to school to get a degree, or starting your own business. These goals require multiple steps and SMART goals along the way.

What sort of mix should you aim for? A great place to start is to identify one long-term goal (make it a really important one!) and two or three short-term goals.

DIFFERENT AREAS OF LIFE

IN CHAPTER 7, we explored the different spheres of life (see page 118). You do not need a goal in every area of your life. In her book *Goddesses in Everywoman*, Jean Shinoda Bolen, MD, explains that people are fulfilled in different ways. She explains that different goddesses are "active" within an individual at any given time. For example, maybe right now you are tapped into your work ethic, your creative talents, or your nurturing caregiver strengths.

Think about which face of the goddess is active for you right now. Flip back in your journal to the goals you jotted down for each life sphere in chapter 7. Meditate on which feel most relevant to you. On a new page, write down one long-term goal at the top of the page, and two or three short-term goals along the sides.

Review the words you have chosen for your goals in your journal and have confidence in your truth. If you need to, reword your thoughts to better match the reality you would like to create for yourself.

For the long-term goal, identify two or three SMART goals that will set you on the right path.

As you begin to work on these goals, speak your words of affirmation (page 55) and revisit your core qualities (page 33) to build your self-worth, self-acceptance, and self-esteem. If they help you, grab your supportive crystals or essentials oils (page 148) to help you when you get stuck.

Your Rainbow Gateway

Chakras are part of your energy body (see page 4). Your chakra system is the bridge to your spiritual self. Pull out your journal; in this fun goal-setting exercise, we will use the chakra bridge to create broad goals in different areas of life.

You'll start with your roots and nurture your way up to sovereignty. As you fill in each chakra, allow the colors and sacred geometry of the chakra to inspire your goals.

Root (Muladhara)
GOAL: *What is your passion? How can you incorporate this passion into your life starting now?*

Sacral (Svadhisthana)
GOAL: *What do you wish to create in this life?*

Solar Plexus (Manipura)
GOAL: *What helps you feel confident and empowered? How can you bring more of this into your life?*

Heart (Anahata)
GOAL: *What do you find beautiful? What heals you? How can you nurture this nature of yourself and radiate it out into the world?*

Throat (Vishuddha)
GOAL: *In what ways do you want to live in your truth?*
How would you like to express yourself?

Third Eye (Ajna)
GOAL: *What is your vision for the future of humanity?*
How will you use your intuition to help get us there?

Crown (Sahasrara)
GOAL: *What will be your crowning glory? Connect to*
your higher self and think big.

STAYING COMMITTED TO YOUR GOALS

NO MATTER WHAT is going on around you, if you are walking
your divine path, you will feel safe on a spiritual level, emotionally secure, and strong in mental clarity. You have done the
work to get here. Now all you have to do is *be* here. Know that
you have everything you need to stay committed to your goals,
even in moments when you may have doubts.

When you are full of self-love and committed to your truth,
you will be resilient to trial and error. Your intuition will serve
as your compass. In fact, you will be able to embrace your
setbacks as part of the process, as reminders to stay the course
rather than turn around. You will also be able to tune out any
perceptions of judgments and projections of others. If someone
says something negative (like maybe they don't think there's
room for another make-up artist), you will stand in your truth,
let it go, and continue on your course.

Remind yourself that with every small step you take, you are
transforming into this resilient, accomplished self.

From time to time, you will inevitably question if you are on
the right path. When this happens, check in with the universe

(see page 76). The universe will send you answers in many forms—you just have to pay attention. When something does catch your attention, instead of taking this symbol at face value, tune into what it triggers inside of you.

For example, maybe you are deciding whether graduate school is the right goal for you. You ask the universe whether it will be worth all that hard work and sacrifice. Later that day, you stumble upon a box of matches that says "green light." Does this trigger a positive feeling inside of you, like *go for it, you've got the green light!* Or does it nudge you to rethink your goal because matches burn, so the sign triggers the feeling that graduate school will just burn all your money away? Two people could receive this exact same symbol and interpret it in contrasting ways according to their own intuition. When interpreting signs, be sure to also check in with your shadows and make sure it's not them talking. Rule out any ways your shadows might be trying to hold you back from succeeding.

You have all the tools you need to stay committed to your goals. When in doubt, revisit previous chapters and journal entries to reclaim your divinity and stay empowered in your truth. Remind yourself of the best possible outcome and believe that you can get there—because you can.

IN HER OWN WORDS:
Stairway to Heaven

Remember that your goals are the steps you take to reach your full potential. To help envision this process, sketch a twisting staircase in your journal. Write your goal at the top, and fill in each step you need to take to get there. You can color in the steps as you complete the goals. It's your own personal stairway to heaven!

Live Your Values

WE EXPLORED THE difference between values and goals in chapter 7 (see page 112), where you also began to identify your values.

Now, imagine that you lived out your values every day as you worked toward your goals. How would your life be different? How would you feel?

Goals are there to inspire us, help us stay focused on what's important to us, and lead us on the right path. Values make up the foundation of the path, carrying us along the way.

DETERMINE YOUR VALUES

Here are some examples of values. Which of these reso-nate with you?

- *Adventure*
- *Ambition*
- *Animal rights*
- *Art*
- *Balance*
- *Beauty*
- *Career*
- *Challenge*
- *Communication*
- *Community*
- *Compassion*
- *Creativity*
- *Environmentalism*
- *Family*
- *Friendship*
- *Generosity*
- *Happiness*
- *Health*
- *Inclusiveness*
- *Justice*
- *Kindness*
- *Love*
- *Loyalty*
- *Mental health*
- *Nature*
- *Peace*
- *Philanthropy*
- *Security*
- *Self-awareness*
- *Service*
- *Tradition*
- *Truth*

In your journal, write down your top five values from the previous list. Now, for each value, brainstorm one way you can recommit to the value if you veer off your path. For example, let's say one of your values is communication, but you got angry and closed yourself off instead of communicating how you felt. Instead of beating yourself up for not living your values, brainstorm a tactic you would use to get back on track, such as apologizing and explaining how you felt in the moment.

Now identify some ways in which your values align with your goals. Revisit the long- and short-term goals you set on page 157, and reflect on the ways your strongly held values will support these goals.

Stay Committed to Yourself

THE BEST PART about a transformative process is that the further you get, the less work you need to do to make a change. You will just . . . be changed. And when that happens, you can relax into enjoying the journey as your true self!

So, as you prepare to emerge, take a moment to believe in yourself. Take one moment, every day, just to believe in yourself: You are emerging with every step you take. Every day is part of the process. How many steps will it take for you to transform?

Before a butterfly can leave its chrysalis, it has to build the strength of its wings. If someone coaxes it out too soon, it will not have the strength to fly. The butterfly gains strength by opening its wings on the *inside*, pushing against its own walls until it can set itself free. Stay true to yourself and your own process, and you will emerge as your true self in your own time, more beautiful than ever.

TIME TO SOAR

START TO OPEN and close your wings. Feel the strength of your spirit and the sovereignty of your soul. Center into your core personal sun and feel your flame burn bright. Invite the element of air to swirl around you. Look to the star-filled night and get ready to take your place in the cosmos. Find your true north star and let the moonlight of your feminine divinity guide your way.

I'll see you there.

A Final Word: On Your Path

IN MY GRADUATE school neuropsychology class, we were given this example: To knock a baseball out of the park, you can't focus too much on your swing. If you overthink it, that will interfere with the nature of how your strength works. So, you practice, strengthen your muscles, hone your techniques, and prepare for the game. You get adequate rest, eat right for your body, and set a goal. When it becomes time to step up to the plate, you focus. You steady yourself. You give yourself a pep talk. You get into your batting stance and look out beyond the stands, because that is where you want the ball to land. The ball comes your way, you give it all you've got, and then you *let go*.

If you try to overcontrol your arm as you swing, it prevents your muscles from acting naturally. It is the physical routine and practice over time that trains the muscles to act with purpose.

As you have developed a routine that works for you, trust that you have everything you need within. You do not need to overthink, because intuition is your friend. By keeping an eye on your goal, being true to your values, and giving it all you've got, you will knock it out of the ballpark!

When you think about how far you've come, always remember what it took to get there. Your results can be

found in the strength you have gained and your soul
growth. Setbacks and obstacles are part of the process.
Getting back up is the hardest part; never underestimate
the courage, faith, and hope you have displayed just for
trying. It is through the process itself that you will see your
true light. When you love yourself and care for yourself,
you are doing your part to heal the world.

ℛesources

Books:

Psychology

Attached: The New Science of Adult Attachment and How It Can Help You Find—and Keep—Love by Amir Levine, MD, and Rachel S. F. Heller, MA

The Drama of the Gifted Child: The Search for the True Self by Alice Miller, PhD

The 5 Love Languages: The Secret to Love That Lasts by Gary Chapman, PhD

Facing Codependence: What It Is, Where It Comes From, How It Sabotages Our Lives by Pia Mellody

Body, Mind, Spirit, and Soul

Eat Right, Feel Right: Over 80 Recipes and Tips to Improve Mood, Sleep, Attention & Focus by Leslie Korn, PhD

The Emotion Code: How to Release Your Trapped Emotions for Abundant Health, Love, and Happiness by Dr. Bradley Nelson

The Empath's Survival Guide: Life Strategies for Sensitive People by Judith Orloff, MD

Focusing by Eugene T. Gendlin, PhD

The Power of Now: A Guide to Spiritual Enlightenment by Eckhart Tolle

Practical Intuition: How to Harness the Power of Your Instinct and Make It Work for You by Laura Day

The Highly Sensitive Person: How to Thrive When the World Overwhelms You by Elaine N. Aron, PhD

The Infinite View: A Guidebook for Life on Earth by Ellen Tadd

Your Story Is Your Power: Free Your Feminine Voice by Elle Luna and Susie Herrick

Auras, Crystals, Chakras, and Essential Oils

Auras: An Essay on the Meaning of Colors by Edgar Cayce

Crystals: The Modern Guide to Crystal Healing by Yulia Van Doren

Essential Aromatherapy: A Pocket Guide to Essential Oils & Aromatherapy by Susan Worwood

Essential Energy: A Guide to Aromatherapy and Essential Oils by Nikki Goldstein

Llewellyn's Complete Book of Chakras: Your Definitive Source of Energy Center Knowledge for Health, Happiness, and Spiritual Evolution by Cyndi Dale

Practical Art of Aromatherapy: Create Your Own Personalized Beauty Treatments and Natural Remedies by Deborah Nixon

The Seven Archetypal Stones: Their Spiritual Powers and Teachings by Nicholas Pearson

The Subtle Body: An Encyclopedia of Your Energetic Anatomy by Cyndi Dale

Websites:

Astrology

Astrolada.com

AstrologyKRS.com

TheNextStep.uk.com/free-birthchart

Health and Well-Being

Chopra.com/articles/what-is-ayurveda

DailyOm.com

DrLeslieKorn.com

Gottman.com

JanetLansbury.com

TheSacredScience.com

ThriveMarket.com

Raise Your Vibration

LouiseHay.com/free-podcast-to-honor-louise
-hays-legacy

YouTube.com/user/TheMeditativeMind

REFERENCES

Ambrose, Kala. *The Awakened Aura: Experiencing the Evolution of Your Energy Body.* Woodbury, MN: Llewellyn Publications, 2011.

American Museum of Natural History. "The Spider Woman." Accessed April 16, 2020. AMNH.org/exhibitions /totems-to-turquoise/native-american-cosmology /the-spider-woman.

Ancient Origins: Reconstructing the Story of Humanity's Past. "Oshun: African Goddess of Love and Sweet Waters." December 25, 2019. Ancient-Origins.net /myths-legends-africa/oshun-african-goddess-love -and-sweet-waters-002908.

Apel, Thomas. "Vesta." Mythopedia. Accessed April 20, 2020. Mythopedia.com/roman-mythology/gods/vesta.

BecVar, Brent, MS. "Introduction to Jyotish: Vedic Astrology." The Chopra Center. November 7, 2013. Chopra. com/articles/introduction-to-jyotish-vedic-astrology.

Berger, Pamela. *The Goddess Obscured: Transformation of the Grain Protectress from Goddess to Saint.* Boston: Beacon Press, 1985.

Bolen, Jean Shinoda. *Goddesses in Everywoman: Powerful Archetypes in Women's Lives.* New York: HarperCollins, 1984.

Cavalli, Thom F. *Alchemical Psychology.* New York: Jeremy P. Tarcher/Putnam, 2002.

The Celtic Journey. "Áine, the Faery Goddess." April 17, 2013. TheCelticJourney.wordpress.com/2013/04/17/aine.

Chevalier, Gaétan, Stephen T. Sinatra, James L. Oschman, Karol Sokal, and Pawel Sokal. "Earthing: Health Implications of Reconnecting the Human Body to the Earth's Surface Electrons." *Journal of Environmental and Public Health* (January 2012). NCBI.nlm.nih.gov/pmc/articles /PMC3265077.

Christ, Carol P. *Rebirth of the Goddess: Finding Meaning in Feminist Spirituality.* New York: Routledge, 1997.

Corbin, Henry. *Spiritual Body and Celestial Earth: From Mazdean Iran to Shi'ite Iran.* Translated by Nancy Pearson. Princeton: Princeton University Press, 1977.

Dale, Cyndi. *Llewellyn's Complete Book of Chakras: Your Definitive Source of Energy Center Knowledge for Health, Happiness, and Spiritual Evolution.* Woodbury, MN: Llewellyn Publications, 2016.

Emoto, Masaru. *The Hidden Messages in Water.* Translated by David A. Thayne. Hillsboro, OR: Beyond Words Publishing, Inc., 2004.

Ensworth, Heather. "Shifts in Consciousness, Earth Changes—Choice Point." January 27, 2020. YouTube video, 32:23. YouTube.com/watch?v=HnE-RjsBVIE &feature=emb_title.

Faulkner, Mary. *Women's Spirituality: Power and Grace.* Charlottesville, VA: Hampton Roads, 2011.

Gendlin, Eugene T. *Focusing.* New York: Bantam Books, 1978.

Goldstein, Nikki. *Essential Energy: A Guide to Aromatherapy and Essential Oils.* New York: Warner Books, 1997.

Gregory, Pam. "New Moon in Aquarius 24th January 2020." January 10, 2020. YouTube video, 20:05. YouTube.com /watch?v=EdtkPYxeGAQ&feature=emb_title.

Gurmukh. *Bountiful, Beautiful, Blissful: Experience the Natural Power of Pregnancy and Birth with Kundalini Yoga and Meditation.* New York: St. Martin's Press, 2003.

Howell, Elizabeth. "Humans Really Are Made of Stardust, and a New Study Proves It." Space.com. January 10, 2017. Space.com/35276-humans-made-of-stardust -galaxy-life-elements.html.

Jung, C. G. *Psychology and Alchemy.* Translated by Gerhard Adler and R. F. C. Hull. Princeton: Princeton University Press, 1953.

Lotzof, Kerry. "Are We Really Made of Stardust?" Natural History Museum. Accessed April 24, 2020. NHM.ac.uk /discover/are-we-really-made-of-stardust.html.

Markale, Jean. *The Great Goddess: Reverence of the Divine Feminine from the Paleolithic to the Present.* Rochester, VT: Inner Traditions, 1999.

Monaghan, Patricia. *The New Book of Goddesses & Heroines.* Woodbury, MN: Llewellyn Publications, 2000.

Nixon, Deborah. *Practical Art of Aromatherapy: Create Your Own Personalized Beauty Treatments and Natural Remedies.* New York: Random House, 1995.

Noble, Vicki. *Shakti Woman: Feeling Our Fire, Healing Our World—The New Female Shamanism*. New York: HarperOne, 1991.

Pearson, Nicholas. *The Seven Archetypal Stones: Their Spiritual Powers and Teachings.* Rochester, VT: Destiny Books, 2016.

PTSD: National Center for PTSD. "How Common is PTSD in Adults?" Accessed March 22, 2020. PTSD.va.gov /understand/common/common_adults.asp.

Reinhart, Melanie. "Chariklo: Wife of Chiron." Accessed March 22, 2020. MelanieReinhart.com/melanie/ Chariklo.htm.

The Recovery Village. "PTSD Facts and Statistics." Updated April 7, 2020. TheRecoveryVillage.com/mental-health /ptsd/related/ptsd-statistics.

Rosicrucian Egyptian Museum. "Deities in Ancient Egypt: Sekhmet." Accessed April 20, 2020. EgyptianMuseum. org/deities-sekhmet.

Thorpe, Penni. "Newly Seeing the Shadow . . . Help!" May 6, 2018. HealingFlowerEnergies.com/2018/05/06 /newly-seeing-the-shadow-help.

Van Doren, Yulia. *Crystals: The Modern Guide to Crystal Healing*. London: Quadrille Publishing, 2017.

Waldherr, Kris. *Embracing the Goddess Within: A Creative Guide for Women*. Hillsboro, OR: Beyond Words Publishing, 1997.

The Wisdom of Kabbalah. "Chapter 1.4: The Awakening of the 'Point in the Heart.'" Accessed April 25, 2020. Kabbalah.info/eng/content/view/frame/37617?/eng /content/view/full/37617&main.

Worwood, Susan. *Essential Aromatherapy: A Pocket Guide to Essential Oils & Aromatherapy.* Novato, CA: New World Library, 1995.

INDEX

G

Generational
wounds, 84
Getting outside of
yourself, 76–78
Gifts
divine, 60–61
shadow, 65–67
sharing, 68, 71
spiritual, 69
Goals, 112–113, 116–118,
155–160
Goddess archetypes,
10, 21–22, 26–32
*Goddesses in
Everywoman*
(Bolen), 157
"Going within," 13, 17
Gregory, Pam, 33
Grief, 84–85
Grounding, 78, 88, 137
Guardian angels, 15, 85

H

Happiness, 143–147
Highly sensitive
persons
(HSPs), 65–66
Honoring others, 37
Hope, 130

I

Intention, 12–15
Interactions with
others, 86–87
Intuition, 35

J

Jung, Carl, 62
Jyotish, 110

K

Karma, 83–84
Kindness, 35
Kowal, Charles, 33

L

Leadership, 66
Letting go, 103–105
Life story, 18–19
Listening to
yourself, 17

M

Maiden aspect, 27
Masculine energy,
26–27, 91
Matron aspect, 27
Mellody, Pia, 104
Mother aspect, 27
Motivational
interviewing,
51–52
interviewing, 51–52

N

Narratives, 18–19
Nature, 77–78, 88–89
Needs, 64–65, 135, 144
Neptune, 54–55
"No," saying, 135

O

Oshun, 130

P

Patience, 18
Perceptions, 101–102
Permission, 97
Persephone, 119

"Point in the
heart," 95–96
Positive qualities, 20.
See also Core
qualities
Post-traumatic
stress disorder
(PTSD), 6–7
Prioritizing yourself,
56–57, 143–147
*Psychology and
Alchemy* (Jung),
62–63

Q

Qi energy, 27, 129

R

Rage, 45
Reframing, 50–52
Reinhart, Melanie, 33
Relationships. *See also*
Boundary-setting
family, 83–85
friendships, 82–83
nurturing, 147
workplace, 85–86
with the world, 92
with yourself, 40–43
Rites of renewal, 63–65

S

Safe, feeling, 100–101
Scotti, James V., 33
Sedna, 33, 117
Sekhmet, 63
Self-awareness, 5–7, 9
Self-care
emotional, 129, 145
importance of, 43,
126–128
intervention, 132

ACKNOWLEDGMENTS

THIS BOOK WAS a cocreation with the universe. I am still in awe of the process of getting to this point, and am so honored to be sharing this time with you. As I am writing this book, Saturn is about to make its three-year transit through Aquarius, from 2020 to 2022. Though the human collective is now experiencing increasingly challenging times, this time may also be the dawning of the Age of Aquarius. May everyone find peace and harmony within themselves and one another by living in their true light and being full of love to usher in this golden age.

I am grateful to my family of origin, extended family, and soul family for their inspiration, guidance, and support. Specific gratitude for my mom's celestial presence in human form, my dad's dedication to the practice of medicine, and my sister, who embodies everything a sister could ever be and more. To my friends who live the true values of sisterhood daily, I am so glad we're in this together. I regularly thank my lucky stars for my husband, his family of fun, love, peace, and harmony, and the little ones who taught me the meaning of Warrior Goddess.

Thank you to all the teachers I have known. From my first grade teacher who recognized daydreaming as a strength, to my high school English teacher who had us reflect on the topics of "intrinsic value" and "man in the cosmos," to my college creative writing teacher, who suggested writing could come from an off-topic philosophical conversation in office hours. Thank you to the preschool and elementary school teachers of my children who inspire us daily. With dedication and kindness, our teachers and school staff plant the seeds for world peace. By maintaining such a beautiful environment for learning, these are the people who are fostering and promoting the values of humanity, creativity, and interconnectedness. They are earth angels in human form.

The final chapters of this book were written during a time of collective uncertainty when we were all "sheltering in place" in the midst of the coronavirus pandemic. I've been reminded, as ever, that in darkness, there is always light. When they are most needed, special spiritual teachers will appear along the way.

Thank you to my spiritual teachers and guardian angels on earth and in the spirit world, for all the faith I will ever need. Universal support and messages of hope and inspiration have come through many interactions on my life path, and I am so grateful for all of them.

To my editor, Samantha, and the team at Callisto Media: This project was so much fun to work on together! It's a dream come true and feels like it was heaven-sent. This book is a testament that when you speak your truth, it just might be carried on angels' wings. Before the recognition of Artemis, in the mountains of provincial Arcadia, lived Callisto. A pre-Hellenic goddess, she ran barefoot through the woods in human form, and also as a mother bear. She represented instinct. When Greek tribes merged her energy with Artemis, Callisto became known as a nymph. No matter how others describe us or perceive us, our true nature remains the same. A very special thank you to Callisto Media and Joe Cho for finding me and giving me the opportunity to write this book. I followed my own instincts to boldly use my voice, and this is one manifestation of that choice. This book has been my friend through these uncertain times, and I hope it becomes yours.

ABOUT THE AUTHOR

DARA GOLDBERG, PHD, is a clinical psychologist who works with women to help them live in their true light at any stage of the life cycle. Through dreamwork and guided meditation, she helps others understand their psychological processes through a spiritual and intuitive lens. Integrating transformational experiences as a natural part of the life journey, she focuses on helping women empower themselves within their own personal circumstances. With recognition of the crucial role early attachment plays in our lives, her services are directed to nurture one's true nature.